What Every Teacher Needs to Know About Assessment

Second Edition

Leslie Walker Wilson

EYE ON EDUCATION
6 DEPOT WAY WEST, SUITE 106
LARCHMONT, NY 10538
(914) 833–0551
(914) 833–0761 fax
www.eyeoneducation.com

Library of Congress Cataloging-in-Publication Data

Wilson, Leslie Walker, 1952-
    What every teacher needs to know about assessment / Leslie Walker Wilson.— 2nd ed.
        p. cm.
    Rev. ed. of: Better instruction through assessment. c2002.
    Includes bibliographical references.
    ISBN 1-930556-89-6
    1. Educational tests and measurements—United States. 2. Students—Rating of—United States. I. Wilson, Leslie Walker, 1952- Better instruction through assessment. II. Title.
    LB3051.W4997 2005
    371.26'0973—dc22

                                                        2004016802

10 9 8 7 6 5 4

Editorial and production services provided by
Richard H. Adin Freelance Editorial Services
52 Oakwood Blvd., Poughkeepsie, NY 12603-4112
(914-471-3566)

Also Available from EYE ON EDUCATION

What Great Teachers Do Differently:
Fourteen Things That Matter Most

Todd Whitaker

What Great Principals Do Differently:
Fifteen Things That Matter Most

Todd Whitaker

The Principal as Instructional Leader:
A Handbook for Supervisors

Sally J. Zepeda

Supervision Across the Content Areas

Sally J. Zepeda and R. Stewart Mayers

Instructional Leadership for School Improvement

Sally J. Zepeda

Dealing with Difficult Teachers, Second Edition

Todd Whitaker

Motivating and Inspiring Teachers:
The Educator's Guide for Building Staff Morale

Todd Whitaker, Beth Whitaker, and Dale Lumpa

Teaching Matters:
Motivating & Inspiring Yourself

Todd and Beth Whitaker

101 "Answers" for New Teachers and Their Mentors:
Effective Teaching Tips for Daily Classroom Use

Annette Breaux

Real Teachers, Real Challenges, Real Solutions
25 Ways to Handle the Challenges of the Classroom Effectively

Annette L. and Elizabeth Breaux

Data Analysis for Continuous School Improvement,
Second Edition

Victoria L. Bernhardt

The Call to Teacher Leadership

Zepeda, Myers, and Benson

**Motivating and Inspiring Teachers:
The Educator's Guide for Building Staff Morale**

Todd Whitaker, Beth Whitaker, and Dale Lumpa

**Achievement Now!
How to Assure No Child Is Left Behind**

Dr. Donald J. Fielder

**Handbook on Teacher Portfolios
for Evaluation and Professional Development**

Pamela D. Tucker, James H. Stronge, and Christopher R. Gareis

**Handbook on Teacher Evaluation:
Assessing and Improving Performance**

James H. Stronge and Pamela D. Tucker

**Handbook on Educational Specialist Evaluation:
Assessing and Improving Performance**

James H. Stronge and Pamela D. Tucker

**Staff Development:
Practices that Promote Leadership in Learning Communities**

Sally J. Zepeda

**Helping Students Graduate:
A Strategic Approach to Dropout Prevention**

Jay Smink and Franklin P. Schargel

Dropout Prevention Tools

Franklin P. Schargel

Strategies to Help Solve Our School Dropout Problem
Franklin P. Schargel and Jay Smink

**At-Risk Students Reaching and Teaching Them,
Second Edition**

Richard Sagor and Jonas Cox

About the Author

Leslie Walker Wilson is Director of Student Assessment and Program Evaluation for the Howard County Public School System in Maryland. While in Howard County, Leslie has been committed to ensuring that teachers understand assessment results so that they can be used to plan effective student instruction. She has presented at a variety of educator's conferences and served as consultant in test score analysis and the interpretation and use of data for a number of school systems in Maryland. Leslie led the committee that designed the first data analysis section of the Maryland State Department of Education's Website. She has taught assessment courses for graduate students at Loyola College and staff development courses sponsored by Howard County. Leslie has authored numerous articles in her fields of expertise, as well as assessment, school improvement, and data interpretation guides and resources for the Howard County Public School System. Previous to her work in Howard County, Leslie was a Specialist in Research and Evaluation at the Maryland State Department of Education where she worked on the design, implementation, and analysis of Maryland's accountability testing program. She holds a master's degree in Community Clinical Psychology from the University of Maryland Baltimore County, where she has served as Alumni Association president. She also holds a Ph.D. in Measurement, Statistics, and Evaluation from the College of Education at the University of Maryland College Park.

Contributors

The following educators provided assistance, consultation, and the student responses used in Chapter 6 from the Howard County Public School System:

Elena Ahr

Leslie Bickner

Sarah Bluth

Marsha Demoree

Eileen Engel

Cindy Evarts

Joan Fox

Amy Green

Barbara Hoffmann

Glenn Heisey

Deborah Jogoda

Julie Jones

Nancy Kalin

Andrea Lang

Kathy Mehalko

Dan Michaels

Lisa Pallett

Roger Plunkett

Anne Schaub

Pat Shrack

Becky Straw

Steve Zagami

Special consultation was provided by Julian Katz and Kay Sammons.

Acknowledgments

In my first book, *Better Instruction Through Assessment: What Your Students Are Trying to Tell You,* I expressed my gratitude to many who supported me, directly and indirectly. This second book became necessary because of the No Child Left Behind Act of 2001. This federal legislation has focused educators on the achievement of *every* student, lifting up the role of quality assessment to new levels of importance. It also adjusted the focus of many accountability programs to the individual student and changed the way we must look at our students' achievement data. I must express my gratitude to my publisher, Robert Sickles, for giving me the opportunity to update my work in alignment with the current educational climate. I also wish to thank my reviewers, who provided thoughtful suggestions and encouragement:

Marcella Emberger, Maryland State Department of Education

Rebecca Harrison, Principal, Amarillo, Texas

Les Potter, Principal, Silver Sands Middle School, Port Orange, Florida

Kathryn Schladweiler, Mason City Community School District, Iowa

As the product of the public education system myself, I owe a debt of gratitude to my former teachers, especially Joy, Jonathan, the University of Maryland Baltimore County, and the University of Maryland College Park. I have always been fortunate to benefit from the encouragement of family, friends, and colleagues. These number many; however, special credit is due my husband Courtney; my loving parents, Jerry and Vern Walker; my grandparents; and my dear friends Carole, Betty, and Sam.

For the good of our society, I believe that education must be about the needs of children, not the needs of adults. As educators, we must approach our chosen profession with honesty and integrity and a focus on children. I am dedicating this book to my family as well as those educators who put children first. Thank goodness there are many. You know who you are.

Leslie Ann Walker Wilson

Table of Contents

Preface

As one of the people who have accepted the responsibility to educate our children, you have chosen a difficult profession. You must balance many different jobs and perform them all effectively. A significant amount of a teacher's time is spent in assessing student progress, and a similar amount of time and some additional stress is associated with the mandated local and state assessments now required in many school systems. These programs may be in addition to the federal testing now required by the No Child Left Behind Act of 2001. In short, every school year an increasing amount of time is devoted to gathering data about what students know and can do, and the quality of the assessments used to do this will determine the quality of the information available to you and your students. Yet, only recently have teacher education programs begun to require teachers to take an assessment course. Those courses tend to either be very technical and difficult for teachers-in-training to understand or consist of a superficial overview of assessment issues (see Stiggins, 2000). Those responsible for the development of teacher education programs share the blame with the measurement community in failing to equip teachers with the skills they need to be confident, accurate assessors and facilitators of their students' learning.

What good is it for states and test publishers to develop and administer assessments that result in valid and reliable information if you, the classroom teacher, cannot understand the results well enough to use them to improve instruction? And what happens when you are responsible for developing, scoring, and interpreting the results of your own tests? Everyone has been the victim of an unfair test or test item. What is needed is an applied approach to a fairly complex subject, which would mean less about theories and formulas and more about how to design and use effective assessments to make sound instructional decisions for students. In essence, what is needed is authentic learning about measurement by all classroom teachers.

Many other resources provide information on the development of good assessment items, including performance tasks as well as the more traditional formats. Still others go into great depth about scoring student responses. But teachers still need help in interpreting the assessment data they have, and making instructional decisions based on this information.

It is the goal of this book to give you a practical understanding of the measurement concepts that you need to make valid and reliable judgments about your teaching and your students' learning. But don't worry! You won't find one formula from that Measurement 101 textbook. Instead, you'll find authentic examples of measurement concepts at work in classrooms and suggestions about how to use what you learn in assessments to improve your students' learning. You will have a chance to practice interpreting assessment results and planning needed instruction.

This book is divided into six chapters. Chapter 1 explores the philosophy of assessment, its purposes, and how it is changing, with attention to the ramifications of the No Child Left Behind (NCLB) Act. We'll discuss issues such as "teaching to the test," mandated assessments for accountability purposes, and the blending of instruction with assessment.

Chapter 2 provides an overview of what teachers need to know about each assessment they administer, a brief introduction to test item formats, and types of scores.

Chapter 3 is a basic, practical introduction to essential measurement concepts such as reliability, validity, item bias, and measurement error. Most important, we'll look at how ignoring these concepts can lead to misinformation about student learning and unnecessary or misguided instruction.

Chapter 4 focuses on practical ways to prepare your students to show what they know without losing precious instructional time. We'll also look at ways teachers can evaluate their own assessments to make them most effective.

Chapter 5 gets to the heart of the matter because it introduces the concept of *threats to validity*, or threats to the accuracy of assessment results. Using actual scenarios, this section demonstrates how to determine if the results are valid for each student, interpret valid assessment results, and, most important, use them to improve your students' learning.

Finally, Chapter 6 provides sample assessment strategies that result in useable student information as well as strategies to address areas of student weakness. Readers will receive some practical experience in *diagnosing* student misconceptions from sample assessment results and *prescribing* instructional interventions.

Along the way, you will have the opportunity to practice what you are learning in the Putting It into Practice sections. You will also gain some of the skills you need to meet some of the professional responsibilities outlined in the very important document developed by the National Council on Measurement in Education. This document, titled *Code of Professional Responsibilities in Educational Measurement* (Schmeiser et al., 1995), outlines the professional responsibilities of anyone who is involved with educational measurement. Teachers must understand and address these responsibilities to competently assess students. This book should help you to meet the requirements of numbers three through seven under "General Responsibilities" in the code:

3. Maintain and improve professional competence in educational assessment.

4. Provide assessment services only in areas of competence and experience, affording full disclosure of professional qualifications.

5. Promote the understanding of sound assessment practices in education.

6. Adhere to the highest standards of conduct and promote professionally responsible conduct within educational institutions and agencies that provide educational services.

7. Perform all professional responsibilities with honesty, integrity, due care, and fairness.

References

Stiggins, R. J., (2000). *Where is our assessment future and how can we get there from here?* Paper presented at the Assessment in Educational Reform: Both Means and Ends Conference, University of Maryland, College Park, MD, June 5–6, 2000.

Schmeiser, C. B., Geisenger, K. F., Johnson-Lewis, S., Roeber, E., and Schafer, W. (1995). *Code of Professional Responsibilities in Educational Measurement*. Washington, DC: National Council on Measurement in Education.

1

Why Do You Need to Know About Assessment?

Teaching has become an even more difficult and demanding profession than ever before. The curriculum gets larger and more complex, compounded with the addition of new objectives to be taught, including all of the new content that used to be taught at home and those topics that previously didn't exist for the majority of school children (HIV, drug use, violence, etc.). Communities expect more out of their schools, and are more actively questioning the quality of student education. Most states have initiated accountability programs to identify ineffective programs or schools. The federal government has passed the No Child Left Behind (NCLB) Act, a complex piece of legislation that includes higher standards for teachers and yearly assessments to demonstrate progress for individual students. Yet with all of these challenges, a tremendous number of dedicated people continue to commit to teach our children. These people will take teaching and learning to new heights in the twenty-first century.

The goal is a more effective educational program for *all* of our students. A good education for every child continues to be the key to the continued growth and success of our society. Students in the United States must be highly educated if they are to effectively compete in an international economy as adults. The fact is that we can, and must provide a good education. First, recent research provides much encouragement for improved student achievement with a paradigm shift in teaching and learning, where good assessment practice is the key (*we can*). Second, the federal government is demanding this improvement and is holding educators increasingly accountable for results by tying federal funding to accountability requirements (*we must*).

The Case for *We Can*

It is true that the children attending our schools today often face more challenges than ever before. For some of them, these challenges become significant barriers to learning. Pallas (1989) defines students as "educationally disadvantaged, if they have been exposed to inadequate or inappropriate educational experiences in the family, school, or community." He goes on to summarize five areas that can put students at risk: poverty, race and ethnicity, family composition, mother's education, and language background. Similar findings were reported by Datcher-Loury (1989), who studied the academic performance of a group of low-income black students. Interviews and observations of the mothers of these students led her to conclude that differences in family behavior and attitudes had significant long-term effects on the students' academic performance. Straits (1987) showed that highly mobile students are also at risk for lower academic achievement. These are but a small sample of the early research studies, but they are representative of the findings.

This research suggests that the challenges students bring to school may be the major determinants of their achievement. However, other recent research suggests that this is not true. It comes from Dr. Bill Sanders, who has shown that the single most important factor in a student's success in school is the teacher. A statistician, Dr. Sanders developed the Tennessee Value-Added Assessment System (Sanders, 2000). This system uses specially designed computer software and years of student test data to analyze the effectiveness of teachers. The program focuses on the gains made by students, so a teacher with low-achieving students will still be rated as "effective" if the students make progress during the school year, regardless of their starting point. The reader is encouraged to read more about this research for a complete understanding of the system, but just a few of Dr. Sanders's and his colleagues' research findings are pertinent to this discussion.

- "Differences in student achievement of 50 percentile points were observed as a result of teacher sequence after only three years." A teacher sequence is three years of effective teachers versus three years of ineffective teachers, given equivalent student ability at the beginning of the three-year sequence.

- "The effects of teachers on student achievement are both additive and cumulative with little evidence of compensatory effects." Once a student has an ineffective teacher, deficits are nearly impossible to eradicate for at least two years. Likewise, once a student has an effective teacher, progress is still evident two years later.

- "As teacher effectiveness increases, lower achieving students are the first to benefit. The top quintile (fifth) of teachers facilitate appropriate to excellent gains for students of all achievement levels." In other words, the best teachers are successful in making progress with students at all levels.

- "Students of different ethnicities respond equivalently within the same quintile of teacher effectiveness." A student's socioeconomic status or ethnicity does not explain differences in achievement as effectively as their teachers' effectiveness.

These conclusions were published as part of a research progress report done by Sanders and Rivers (1996).

One of the keys to improved student achievement is a focus on individual students and their instructional needs. During the 2000–2001 school year, Superintendent John O'Rourke of the Howard County Public School System in Maryland asked for the names of all third graders who were reading below grade level. This important question sparked additional questions and ultimately served to focus the attention of the Howard County Public School System on the achievement of every child, in a foreshadowing of the NCLB legislation. Superintendent O'Rourke's request also inspired an initiative known as Student Support Plans.

Although this initiative began with the basic identification of struggling students, it quickly took the next logical step to actively address these students' needs. Student Support Plans are individualized instructional plans designed to address the specific weaknesses in reading and/or mathematics for students designated as working below grade level in those content areas. In order for students working below grade level to catch up with their on-grade-level peers, they must make more than a year's growth in one year. Student strengths and weaknesses are identified, and research-based strategies are implemented to target instruction to meet individual student needs. These strategies may include a variety of formats, including interventions during the regular school day, after school, or in a summer program.

The Student Support Plan initiative has since become an integral part of Howard County's Comprehensive Plan for Accelerated School Improvement, and it is resulting in students making more than one year's growth in one year. Results at the end of the 2002–2003 school year (the end of grade 5) showed that a total of 197 of the 460 students in the original cohort were reading on or above grade level. This was an improvement for 43 percent of the students. A total of 123 (27 percent) of these students had been reading on or above grade level since the end of grade 4. Similarly, at the end of fifth grade, 78 of the 242, or 33 percent, of the original cohort of students were working on or above grade level. This was an overall improvement for 32 percent of the cohort students. These preliminary results suggest that with a focus on individual students and their instructional needs, *we can* improve student achievement.

What do the students themselves tell us? In 1993, the Howard County Public School System conducted a study to determine what some of the differences were between their high- and low-achieving students. The students' responses suggested that the differences between the high and low achievers are not a factor of ethnic group or socioeconomic status, but are related to differences in academic values, expectations, and the commitment behaviors demonstrated. Higher percentages of high-achieving students reported that their parents knew how they were doing in school. These higher achievers also demonstrated more commitment behaviors such as completing homework and other assignments on time, and persisting with difficult schoolwork. These students also perceived their teachers as having high expectations for them. The lower-achieving students did not perceive their teachers as having high expectations for them or calling on them as often as high-achieving students. Although 96 percent of students reported that their parents think that school is important, and 88 percent are expected to get good grades, only 61 percent think it is important to work hard in school. Some students do not see a link between the effort they put into their school work and their grades. Only 67 percent believed they would get better scores on a test if they studied for it.

These findings suggest the possibility that some students do not believe the assessments they are given accurately assess what they have learned—in other words, the students believe that the assessments are not valid. The findings also suggest that students do not believe that they have sufficient information or control to improve their performance. Although research supports the need for positive involvement from parents, teachers, and students, as well as high expectations and encouragement from parents or family, it also suggests that many answers can be found in the classroom. This is good news! When we empower all students to engage meaningfully in the learning process, we will unlock the gates to learning for all students.

Be the Best You Can Be

It can be frightening to learn that, even with all of the challenges facing students today, their teachers are still the single most important factor in student academic growth rates. All teachers want their students to succeed, but many teachers do not know how to improve their students' achievement. This can be partially attributed to the fact that most teacher-training programs include little, if any, coursework in assessment. (Cizek, 2000; Schafer & Lissitz, 1987; Stiggins, 1999) Yet, as a teacher, you cannot possibly be effective if you do not have the skills to determine your students' instructional needs. You will spend a good third of your time assessing your students. You assess their needs almost automatically when they ask or answer a question. You observe them in the classroom as they work on assignments. You develop their assignments and evaluate their work. You make up tests and assign grades. You comment on students' writing and provide feedback. And the way a teacher assesses students and provides feedback will greatly influence student learning. What activity could be more important?

So what can you, as the teacher, do? First, forget about all of the things you cannot change about your students or their circumstances and concentrate on what you can change: your teaching. You can always improve your instruction by making it more responsive to your students' needs. Assessment is the tool you will use to involve your students in helping you to determine those needs. Second, to become the most effective teacher you can be, you must be familiar with assessment: what it is, how to do it, and most importantly, how to interpret and use the results. This book will help you to accomplish this.

Assessment

Because assessment is so important, we first need to explore its definition. The Merriam-Webster Dictionary (1997) defines "assessment" as follows:

> *n* 1: the act or instance of assessing; 2: an amount assessed.

Assessment is a relatively new word in education; even the dictionary does not include a definition relevant to education. The main source of information about what students had learned used to be the *test*. Now, teachers use many sources of information to determine what their students have learned, thus the more generic term, *assessment*.

Assessment can include any activity that serves to provide feedback to the teacher and students about what the student has learned. Examples are the more traditional test items (multiple-choice, short answer, or matching); constructed response items (where students respond to a prompt requiring them to organize their thoughts, take a stand and support it, provide an explanation); or a project or performance task (requiring students to write and give a speech, write an article or develop a brochure, design a lesson for younger students). The more variety used in assessment, the more complete the picture of what the students know and can do. In their book *Understanding by Design,* Wiggins and McTighe (1998) provide a very complete discussion of the different types of assessment, and how to choose a type appropriate for a given lesson. An important premise of their discussion is that the assessment is designed *before* the lesson. The teacher must determine what the students must be able to do at the conclusion of the lesson *prior* to determining the best instructional strategies to use to accomplish that goal. Standards for determining the quality of the student work must also be established.

Teaching versus Learning

In his book, *Student-Involved Classroom Assessment* (2001), Richard Stiggins provides an historical perspective on testing during the last century. The evolution from test to assessment has come about in a series of steps, and with a shift in paradigm—in the way we think about gathering and using information about students' learning.

First, a test defined a fairly constrained set of questions. Each question had a correct answer, and a grade on the test was simple to compute. The purpose of the test was, in fact, to assign a grade to the student, and, in most cases, to rank order students. This grade served as a final, summative evaluation of the student's performance and generally was determined by how the class had performed as a whole. If a student performed at the top of the class, that student received a high grade. This *norm-referenced* ranking meant that by definition, some students would fail. This process often caused a disconnect—the teachers taught, but according to the test results, students didn't learn. Faced with low test scores, the teacher's typical response might have been "But I taught this." The next day, class would proceed as usual.

But some out-of-the-box thinkers began to question that response. And in fact, effective teachers were beginning to do much more. *These teachers, who truly had as their purpose that students learn the curriculum, began to use the students' test results as feedback on the effectiveness of their teaching. Faced with low test scores, their typical response would be "I taught this, but apparently, my students did not learn it. I need to look at their assessment results to learn what types of additional instruction they need, and provide that instruction."*

Because these teachers knew the objective of education is that students learn, they began to modify the instruction they provided to increase their students' learning. These teachers were not concerned with rank-ordering their students, but they were concerned with making sure every student gained the skills being taught. Given the increasing demands of this new century, this *criterion-referenced* approach fits more appropriately with the goals of education. In other words, to be successful, all students must attain a high level of skills, so the classroom goal is no longer to rank-order, but to bring all students to mastery, and to move as many students as possible well beyond that point.

This distinction between *teaching* and *learning* is an important one. Teaching without learning is a worthless exercise; therefore, the assessment of whether or not students have learned becomes integral to the process of education. Teaching is merely a process we use to obtain our goal of learning, which is the desired outcome. Assessment is the process used to determine whether or not the outcome was met. To be meaningful, the teacher must establish a smooth flow of instruction blended with assessment and actively use the assessment results to assist students to improve their performance.

The Evolution of Change

In many instances, the test information teachers had was not detailed enough to assist them in determining how they should change their instruction. To do that more effectively, they needed to modify the way they gathered information about their students. Many of the test formats used previously (multiple-choice, true-false, matching, etc.) were just not effective at helping them to identify the misconceptions or gaps in knowledge the students had. These item formats were designed to produce a quick, objective score, usually correct or incorrect. They yielded little opportunity to see the source of the students' errors or to allow students to explain their thinking. The only available information was that the item was answered incorrectly. The reason for the incorrect response was assumed to be that the student has not mastered the content being assessed.

Another limitation peculiar to published standardized tests is that the results are often not available until several weeks after the test is administered. This means that errors in student thinking or incorrect information have been allowed to persist (and perhaps be practiced) for extended periods.

In addition, test item formats were constantly being criticized for their lack of association with how students would ultimately use the information being tested. This has become even more of an issue with the emphasis on the extension of learning. Students need more than basic skills and knowledge to be successful in today's world. Curricula now include objectives relating to the application of skills to problem solving, the development of critical thinking skills and the use and processing of information. The assessment of these skills requires different techniques in addition to the methods used in the past. After all, in the workplace it is rare to be asked a question and, rather than being asked to provide an answer, be given four alternatives from which to select. And when was the last time you asked your physician a matching question? This is not to say that these formats do not have a place in today's assessments. Besides being efficient and easy to score accurately, multiple-choice items can be designed, with some effort, to measure higher-order thinking. Although ultimately students may be selecting from four answer choices, they may have had to perform several problem-solving steps before arriving at the point of selecting their answer.

The point is that when we change the focus of instruction, assessment must change, too. Authentic learning requires authentic assessment. These newer methods require students to show what they know in a realistic setting by asking them to analyze science experiments, make predictions, work in groups to solve a problem, and so forth. Sometimes, the assessment is changed to force a change in instruction.

This happened in Maryland, where a performance assessment was designed to model good instruction. This assessment required students to use manipulatives in mathematics, such as spinners and dice; in science, students performed experiments and wrote about what they learned and how their hypotheses changed. The test was constructed response (students composed all of their responses), and tasks were integrated to provide authentic problem scenarios (i.e., a given task may include questions about math, science, social studies, and students may be scored on their writing and language usage while responding to a social studies or science question). This test made instruction in Maryland schools more hands-on, more integrated, and involved more problem-solving, critical thinking, and application of skills. The test has since been modified to meet the requirements of NCLB legislation, but it maintained some of its problem-solving and authentic characteristics. For more information about the Maryland assessment, log on to the Web site at www.mdk12.org.

A system such as that in Maryland and other states causes a true blending of instructional activities with assessment activities. Students can be learning during preassessment activities (while performing experiments, reading, etc.) But sometimes, the activities that follow will be instructional; other times the teacher will step out and require the students to solve problems individually on their own. It is these times that the instructional activity becomes an assessment activity instead. Nevertheless, the result is that when students take an assessment, they do not see much difference between the assessment and the kind of instructional activities in which they participate every day.

The addition of these more authentic item types and tasks to the teacher's collection of assessment tools provides much more flexibility in the way students can be assessed. And teachers have more information about what their students can and cannot do. As the student body becomes more and more diverse, different students will need different kinds of instruction. Isn't it natural, then, to expect that they need different kinds of assessment? Everyone has heard of someone (perhaps even themselves) who is "not a good test taker." We do not say that the person has not learned anything, only that they are not a good test taker. Alternative methods to allow students to show what they have learned assist a teacher in making accurate judgments about all of their students, as well as determine their instructional needs.

Assessment is something that is integral to the role of the teacher, and most teachers are experts in assessment. They spend most of their day doing it, but it comes so naturally that they don't define it as assessment. Consider the following scenario: The teacher poses a question to the students and blank stares result. The teacher rephrases the question. Students provide meaningful answers, but the answers are not in depth. The teacher asks for more information. The students are unable to provide an in-depth response supported by details. The teacher designs a follow-up lesson that includes some scaffolding to help students see how to construct better responses. This is an example of a teacher quickly processing information received from the students and making a modification in instruction to accommodate the need revealed during the informal assessment.

Summary

The work by Stiggins, Wiggins, McTighe, and others is part of a large body of teaching, learning, and assessment information, mostly generated in the last 10 years by some creative and enlightened educators. The research shows that teachers can and do facilitate improvement in student learning. You will find an annotated bibliography at the end of this book that can serve as a resource in your quest for more detailed information about the excellent work of these people. As you extend your reading, you will become convinced that *we can* do much more to enhance student learning, even with all of the challenges we face. You will also come to realize that much of our success depends on arming teachers with practical knowledge about how to assess students and how to use those results to improve instruction. This book may well be the first step in that process.

The Case for *We Must*—No Child Left Behind

An important step in the evolution from test to assessment has been the advent of accountability programs. Although accountability programs are not new to the teachers in most states in the United States, the NCLB Act significantly raises the stakes and the expectations for all states, local school districts, and schools. Briefly, this act, signed into law by President Bush in January 2002, provides for stronger accountability for student achievement results, increased flexibility and local control of federal school funding, expanded educational options for parents, and an emphasis on teaching methods proven to be successful. The legislation is complex and touches on many aspects of education. For states to receive federal funding for education, they must meet the requirements of NCLB. Teachers need to be most familiar with the accountability testing and corresponding requirements for *adequate yearly progress* (AYP), and the criteria for *highly qualified* teachers. To meet the highly qualified criteria, teachers of core subject areas must be fully state certified by the end of the 2005–2006 school year. New teachers must meet these criteria to be hired. For your state's specific criteria, contact your State Department of Education.

In addition, each state has been charged with developing an accountability system to meet federal guidelines. These systems require

♦ Statewide standards and assessments in reading, mathematics, and science

♦ Individual assessments to be administered annually in each of grades 3–8 and once in grades 10–12

♦ State AYP reports (state, district, and school level)

♦ Disaggregated data reporting for poverty, race/ethnicity, disability, and Limited English Proficiency

♦ Academic options for students in low-performing schools through supplemental instruction or school choice

The concept of adequate yearly progress is central to the NCLB Act. Although states have been charged with defining AYP, they must set their goals so that *all* students in *all* subgroups in *all* districts and schools make steady and consistent progress and meet state proficiency standards by the 2013–2014 school year. AYP is based on reading and mathematics achievement and one other indicator (for high schools that indicator must be graduation rate). A science requirement will be added in the near future. To make AYP, schools, districts, and states must include 95 percent of their students in their assessment programs. All subgroups must make AYP for the school to make AYP. This includes students with disabilities and students with limited English proficiency. A school not making AYP for two consecutive years enters school improvement during which they must develop or modify a school improvement plan, and offer all students school choice. If improvement does not occur, the school must continue the above and offer supplemental educational services to all students from low-income families. The process is outlined for a five-year plan, ending in total restructuring of the school if it does meet AYP requirements.

This is a very abbreviated and incomplete synopsis of the NCLB requirements. Log on to www.ed.gov for more complete information.

What No Child Left Behind Means to the Teacher

Besides the obvious requirements for teacher certification, this new legislation has some far-reaching implications for teachers. Because students must meet proficiency at each grade level, the expectation is that each student will make at least one year's growth in one year. The monitoring of this will be facilitated by the design of yearly tests, and student progress (or lack of it) can be linked to individual teachers. A positive for teachers is the availability of data to self-evaluate effectiveness. But there will be significant challenges. No longer can the pace of instruction be slowed for certain groups of students, who end the school year completing only three-quarters of the curriculum. Every student must be instructed in the entire year's curriculum, and every student will take the same assessment. There are no lower standards for students with disabilities or other challenges. Students who are currently behind must have their instruction accelerated so that they can become proficient. This means they may have to make *more* than one year's progress in a year. And with the requirement to test 95 percent of students, there will be no allowance to excuse the low-achieving student from the assessment.

The obvious question on all of our minds is where will we get the time for this? Although some schools are masters at finding additional instructional time for students who need it, others will need to be creative. Some students may need additional instructional time during the regular school day, and this may impact their extracurricular activities or free time. Still others may need extended school days, and an extended school year. Regardless of where the time is found, the most obvious message from NCLB is that *every* student counts. *We must* educate *every* student, one student at a time.

Living with Accountability

Educational accountability elicits many emotional reactions. This direction has certainly taken some of the autonomy away from schools because they must answer to another authority for the job they are doing. The idea that teachers may be held accountable for what their students learn, or don't learn, may be threatening. Newspapers and TV reporters provide us with story after story of teachers or administrators who felt so much pressure that they were compelled to cheat on tests so that their students' performance met standards. Others are bitter because they are forced to "teach to a test." Schools are continually ranked and rated publicly, an activity that does nothing to improve the performance of schools with low-achieving students. Real estate agents sell neighborhoods and houses based on which schools the children living there would attend.

Very few newspaper articles, TV reports or state-generated reports of the results of such programs talk about the inherent limitations of these accountability programs. First, no assessment can do it all, there is always a major purpose for each test, but people want it to do more. Take, for example, the state that has a test designed to evaluate the implementation of the curriculum for school accountability purposes. Before long, someone will want to use that test to rank schools, evaluate students and teachers, determine rewards and sanctions, and so on. These are all inappropriate uses of a single test designed to provide a limited measure of curriculum implementation. Each assessment is a snapshot of the student achievement in that school, but it does not provide a complete evaluation. Each school is a unique community, with its own special accomplishments and problems, positives and limitations. Providing standardized information about schools can be useful if data on relevant other indicators can receive the same emphasis as the test scores. Every piece of information provides an important piece to the puzzle, but we must have all of those pieces to have a complete picture.

The Benefit of Assessment-Literate Teachers

What is often lost in the emotion of accountability programs is the belief that data can help schools to improve. Assessment results are important data. In his book *Results* (1999), Mike Schmoker observes "most schools still do not conscientiously examine the number of students who can do such activities as problem-solve, analyze, calculate, and compose and then (2) adjust instruction and programs accordingly." Yet Schmoker provides numerous useful examples of schools that do just that, and their students experience growth and improvement. The key is to have a staff of assessment-literate teachers, who can monitor their students' progress and use instructional strategies to ensure continual growth and improvement for each student. Teachers must learn to use data as well as, or better than, the public who are becoming increasingly sophisticated in using data themselves. To do anything less is to weaken the teaching profession. To not embrace the accountability movement is for us to reject the same high standards we expect of our doctors, lawyers, bankers, stockbrokers, and other professionals.

A Call to Action

Teachers cannot continue to be surprised and frustrated by their students' results on standardized tests used for accountability. *We must* take the lead, and not be defeated by the data, but learn from it, and act on it. Teachers who are literate in assessment will not be victims of accountability systems. They will know how to use data to improve student learning and be successful with teaching and accountability. They will know where their students stand because they will have accurate data about each student's progress. And they will be able to use that data to make sure their students reach new learning heights, through improved instruction.

This book presents topics that will enable you to be a successful *participant* in accountability programs (not a *victim*) by helping you become the best teacher you can be. A significant part of being that teacher means you will understand the most important measurement issues and how to respond to them. The mystery will be gone from the mandated tests, your students will be learning, and the accountability programs will take care of themselves.

Exploring Attitudes toward Tests

Before we get started, let's explore some attitudes toward some of the mandated tests being used for accountability. Many times, teachers complain that because of these assessments they must teach to a test. Parents hearing this are upset and think the test is compromising their child's education. Is this always the case? Is teaching to a test always a bad thing?

Consider this scenario. Mr. Katz is your son's very enthusiastic and effective world history teacher. He is fascinated with ancient Roman civilization and spends the bulk of the school year teaching it. However, the school's curriculum requires students to study a broad spectrum of world history, and the students in Mr. Katz's class do not receive that content coverage. If the school has a test to assess whether or not students have learned the curriculum, Mr. Katz's students will probably not do well on any section but ancient Roman history. They have not been exposed to the entire curriculum. In fact, your son may have an as-yet undiscovered passion for the French Revolution, but he will not even be introduced to it.

When approached with these problems, Mr. Katz is likely to grumble about being asked to teach to a test, but is what he was doing really best for his students? If the only way Mr. Katz will teach the entire curriculum is because of a test, then that test may be a good thing for his students. The test helps to make sure that there is some kind of standardization, but it does not have to limit creativity. The important thing is to teach all you can to all of your students, do it well, and be sure to cover the essentials.

Teaching to the Test

The concept of teaching to a test always seems to come with negative connotations. It is often thought of as cheating. However, teaching to the test and cheating are two very different things. Teachers are expected to teach their students the skills and concepts they will need to meet the challenges of tests. But they are not to give their students an unfair advantage over others by providing them with information they should not have prior to testing. We will explore some of the issues associated with teaching to a test. Take the following quiz. In the space provided, enter a "TT" if you think the activity is teaching to the test. Enter a "C" if you think the activity is cheating.

Quiz

_____ 1. Teaching students the skills they need to perform well on the test

_____ 2. Providing students with practice on actual test items

_____ 3. Providing students with practice on items similar to the ones on the test

_____ 4. Giving students the answers to items on the test

_____ 5. Discussing the content of actual test items with students prior to the test

_____ 6. Being familiar with tested content, and teaching the related curriculum

_____ 7. Changing the order of instructional units once you see what is to be covered on the test

Now let's discuss these activities.

1. Certainly number one is teaching to the test; basically, you are teaching what the students need to know to perform well. But is it cheating? Why would we give students an assessment on material they had not been taught? Assessment is not a game we play with students; it is a method for acquiring data about what they know and can do, so that we can provide them with further needed instruction.

   The real issue here is whether or not the assessment is worth teaching to. If the assessment does not measure skills and knowledge that we want our students to have, then the assessment is not valuable. But if the assessment measures student achievement on a valued skill, the expectation is that we will teach the students that skill, then assess them to see that they have learned it. Assume for a minute that you are a first grade teacher and your math curriculum specifies you are to teach the students how to add single digits. You teach the students how to add, then you give them a test consisting of single digit addition problems. You taught to the test, but isn't that the point? This is not cheating, and it is definitely not a negative aspect of assessment.

   Often, you will hear teachers complain that they have to teach something *because* it is on a test. If a test is the only reason that students are taught concepts such as graphing data, writing hypotheses, genres in literature, or the Pythagorean theorem, then thank goodness for the test! However, if the test assesses skills not valued by the community or stressed in the curriculum, the teachers' frustration is understandable.

   (Answer: TT)

2. Providing students the opportunity to practice actual test items is outright cheating. Some may try to justify it as teaching to the test, because the activity provides the students with instruction along with their practice. At least teaching to the test implies that some instruction occurred! Students who know the content and have the skills they need do not need to see the actual test items before the test. They will be able to apply what they have been taught to these new problems, and perform well on the test without prior knowledge of the actual items.

    (Answer: C)

3. Providing students with practice on items similar to the ones on the test is a good way to prepare students for a test. Students become familiar with the item types and the strategies for approaching them. But an effective teacher will give students a variety of item types, not just those on the "test of the month" to make sure that students are developing their problem-solving and thinking skills. Technically, this is teaching to the test, particularly the test item format, but it is not cheating. It becomes a problem when this type of test preparation takes precedence over teaching the curriculum, so it must be incorporated into regular classroom instruction. A particularly effective way to familiarize students with a variety of item formats is to use a different type for each day's warm-up activity. See Chapter 4 for further information.

    (Answer: TT)

4. Giving students the answers to items on the test? This strategy doesn't involve any teaching to the test. It is just cheating—plain, simple, and wrong. Teachers willing to provide students with answers to test items must evaluate their moral and ethical standards and make sure their actions are determined by what is best for their students. Students who would need to be given answers to tests to perform well need and deserve additional instruction. Providing students with answers is also inadvisable for job security, because more often than not, one or more students will see the wrong in this practice and confide to an adult, making this type of test preparation quite risky.

    (Answer: C)

5. Discussing the content of actual test items with students prior to the test can involve some instruction or hints. If it does either, it is cheating. Teachers are often frustrated that their instruction may

not have included the same vocabulary or presentation that is used on the test. Therefore, they feel that even though their students know the material being assessed, they may not recognize what the test question is asking. In classroom assessment, it is perfectly reasonable for you to clarify a question that students do not understand. This will make it a more valid assessment. However, on a standardized test, all students must have the same testing experience. This experience is not going to include discussion of actual test items for all students being tested in other classrooms and other schools; therefore, it is cheating.

The best way to make sure your students are familiar with the vocabulary used on the test is for you to vary the way you phrase your questions so students have a wide assessment vocabulary. It also helps for you to be familiar with the writing style of the standardized assessments your students will encounter. That way, you can write similar questions, using similar language and style for your own assessments. You can also use this style and vocabulary when asking your students to respond to questions you may ask orally. That way, when they see the test items, they will be comfortable with the way the items are written.

(Answer: C)

6. Being familiar with tested content and teaching the related curriculum is teaching to the test! It is also your job! However, it is not cheating. Like item 1, if the test assesses skills that we value and want students to have, it is worth administering. If the test is worth giving, then it is worth aligning the curriculum to cover the content assessed on the test. Then it is the teacher's responsibility to teach the students the content they need to help them perform well on the test. And the test gives us information about how well we taught the curriculum and, therefore, how well the students learned.

(Answer: TT)

7. Any time a teacher makes changes in planned instruction because of advance knowledge about an assessment, that teacher is most likely cheating. For many schools, and in several content areas, the order of units to be taught is unimportant. For example, the electricity unit in science does not have to be taught before inertia. They are unrelated topics. In fact, often it is necessary for different classes of students to be studying different units because of insufficient materials to have everyone doing

the same thing at once. This is common for English classes when two classes will be reading *The Great Gatsby* while another class is reading *The Scarlet Letter.* But given that standardized mandated assessments may be given prior to the end of the school year, it is expected that part of the curriculum will not have been covered by testing time. Unfortunately, this is the luck of the draw. Sometimes, what is emphasized on the test will have been taught, sometimes not. But adjustments in the curriculum should not be made solely because of advance information about an assessment. That would be giving students an unfair advantage that is not available to all test takers.

(Answer: C)

Hopefully, this exercise has helped you to see the difference between teaching to the test and cheating. Unfortunately, much education of the public must take place before they will understand that teaching to the test is not necessarily bad, and it is certainly not synonymous with cheating. Do your part! Discuss this issue within your school and with your students' parents. An article by Dr. W. James Popham that could be used to help present these issues in your school appeared in the March 2001 issue of *Educational Leadership.*

It Is All about Classroom Assessment

The meaningful day-to-day assessment of students will be accomplished in the classroom, not by a standardized test. Standardized tests will most likely validate the results of classroom assessments, but because of the time required for scoring and reporting, standardized tests are less likely to be used for day-to-day instructional planning. Therefore, classroom assessments take on an important, prominent role in the educational process. Because of this role, they must meet high quality standards.

Consider the following quote from Richard Stiggins (1999, p. 27):

> "The differences between sound and unsound classroom assessment, record keeping, and communication strategies are clear and nonnegotiable. If teachers do not understand how to produce quality assessments and use them well, their students are placed directly in harm's way. Because the academic well-being of the student hangs in the balance, excellence in classroom assessment is a must."

In classroom assessment, typically the teacher makes up the test. That means that no student should be administered a classroom assessment containing material that the student has not been taught. However, classroom assessments are not guaranteed to be clear, unambiguous, fair, unbiased, and result in valid scores. Although classroom assessment is by far the most important assessment, the assessment that is most relevant to the students and parents, as well as the assessment that will drive a teacher's instruction, all of the resources to assure quality are spent on the state-mandated testing and the test publishers' tests. The remainder of this book is an attempt to address the issues of assessment quality, with an emphasis on score interpretation. Many references already exist to assist the teacher in item construction, scoring, and other test development skills. We will emphasize the interpretation of assessment results and discuss test item and scoring quality only to the extent that it impacts the interpretation of test results.

In Chapter 2, we will explore some of the details you need to know about the assessments you administer. This chapter will provide the background information you will need to learn about any assessment you will give, and it will also give you a framework for what issues you should consider when making up your own classroom assessments and discussing them with your students. You can use your own assessments to help prepare your students to be successful on standardized assessments too. Although the design and development of classroom assessments is beyond the scope of this book, the bibliography contains some good resources that will help you to strengthen your skills in that area.

Summary

This chapter has touched on some of the most controversial and emotional topics in education today. Regardless of your level of support for the NCLB legislation, or your comfort with the concepts of accountability and assessment, these are realities with which educators must cope. Hopefully, this chapter has given you some new perspectives to discuss with your colleagues and community.

References

Cizek, G. L. (2000). Pockets of resistance in the assessment revolution. *Educational Measurement: Issues and Practice, 19*(2), 16–23.

Datcher-Loury, L. (1989). Family background and school achievement among low income blacks. *Journal of Human Resources, 24*(3), 528–544.

Pallas, A. (1989). *Making schools more responsive to at-risk students.* East Lansing, MI: Center for Research on Teacher Learning. (ERIC Digest No. 60)

Popham, W. J. (2001). Teaching to the test. *Educational Leadership, 58*(6), 16–20.

Sanders, W. L. (2000). *Perspectives: Value-added assessment and effective teaching.* Paper presented at the Baltimore Metropolitan Area Collaborative Conference, Columbia, MD.

Sanders, W. L. (2000). Value-added assessment from student achievement data: Opportunities and hurdles. *Journal of Personnel Evaluation in Education*, 14(4), 329–339.

Sanders, W. L., & Rivers, J. (1996). *Cumulative and residual effects of teachers on future student academic achievement.* Research Progress Report, University of Tennessee Value-Added Research and Assessment Center.

Schafer, W. D., & Lissitz, R. W. (1987) Measurement training for school personnel: Recommendations and reality. *Journal of Teacher Education,* 38, 57–63.

Schmoker, M. (1999). *Results* (2nd ed.). Alexandria, VA: Association for Supervision and Curriculum Development.

Stiggins, R. J. (2001). *Student-involved classroom assessment* (3rd ed.). Upper Saddle River, NJ: Merrill Prentice Hall.

Stiggins, R. J. (1999) Evaluating classroom assessment training in teacher education programs. *Educational Measurement: Issues and Practice, 18*(1), 23–27.

Straits, B. C. (1987). Residence migration and school progress. *Sociology of Education, 60*(1), 34–43.

Wiggins, G., & McTighe, J. (1998). *Understanding by design.* Alexandria, VA: Association for Supervision and Curriculum Development.

2

What You Must Know about the Assessments You Administer

Know Your Standardized Tests

As the instructional leader of the classroom, you have many responsibilities. One of them is learning about the assessments you must administer to your students. Teachers must be well informed about any standardized assessment that the students will be taking because it is the teacher's responsibility to educate students, and sometimes parents, about these assessments. The teacher must be well trained in test security and administration procedures to maintain the integrity and validity of assessment results. Currently, most school systems require some form of standardized testing. As a result of No Child Left Behind (NCLB)legislation, most states have similar or additional testing requirements to those required by school districts.

Another teacher responsibility is to prepare the students for such assessments. First, preparation for a valued assessment means the students will learn important information and skills. Second, you want the test results to be a valid indicator of what the students know and can do. This chapter will show you what you need to know about the standardized assessments your students will be administered to prepare them to do their best. A later chapter will give you additional practical ways to prepare your students for any assessment through regular classroom instruction and activities.

We will start with a definition. A standardized test consists of a set of items administered to all students, under the same conditions, scored in the same way, and with results interpreted in the same way. Because every tested student is treated in exactly the same way, the test is said to be *standardized*. These standardized conditions allow comparisons to be made between students and groups of students.

Purpose

First and foremost, teachers must be aware of the purpose of the standardized assessment. The purpose of the assessment will determine the importance it is given in instruction, and how it is interpreted and used by the teacher, the school, and the parents. Let's explore some of the more common purposes for local and state-mandated assessment:

- To provide a standardized measure of achievement
- To report school scores as a measure of school accountability (i.e., to meet NCLB requirements)
- To make comparisons of school or student achievement to other schools or students
- To certify students for progression to the next grade or to graduate from high school
- To identify students for possible participation in special programs

These purposes can be accomplished with two different types of standardized tests. Tests can be either *norm-referenced* or *criterion-referenced*, or in a more creative approach, both. A norm-referenced test ranks, or orders, students by comparing them to others. The test is given to a group, called the *norm group*, that is representative of students expected to take the test. In most cases, this group will be representative of the population of the United States. Several types of scores are derived from the performance of the norm group. We will discuss some of these later in this chapter. The purpose of the norm-referenced test is to compare student performance against that of the norm group. The student with a high score on a norm-referenced test has performed better than many of the students in the norm group. The student who performs at the same level of the average student in the norm group will receive an average score. The student whose performance is below that of most of the students in the norm group will receive a low score.

The criterion-referenced test compares student performance to a standard. Its purpose is not to rank order, but to classify students. A standard is set, for example for satisfactory or excellent, pass or fail performance, and each student's score is compared to that standard (the cut score). As you can understand, it is possible for all students to pass, or for all students to fail. The criterion-referenced test does not spread students out in a distribution the way a norm-referenced test does.

Both types of tests serve a purpose, but each purpose is different. So it is important for the teacher to know whether the test to be administered to their students is norm-referenced or criterion-referenced, that is, whether the students are to be rank-ordered, or compared to a standard.

Because both norm-referenced and criterion-referenced tests have advantages, and the main difference between them is interpretation of the results, there is nothing to prevent the use of a test for both purposes. A test can be administered to a norm group and scores can be derived to compare student performance to that group, and at the same time, a cut score or criterion can be established that is relevant to the standards being assessed. Results yield information about how the students measure up to a standard as well as how they compare to the norm group.

Obviously, the more that is riding on the test results for the student, the more high stakes the test is. A test administered to certify students for high school graduation is more important than one administered to give parents and teachers an idea of where the student's achievement ranks among other students. The consequences are far more serious for poor performance on the high stakes test. However, some assessments serve more than one purpose. The assessment administered to provide parents with individual student feedback can also be used to evaluate a school. Therefore, the assessment that seems less important to the individual student may be of great importance to the school. Depending on the state, NCLB tests are very high stakes for schools and school systems because they determine adequate yearly progress. But these same tests may or may not have high-stakes consequences for individual students. Parents can be frustrated by the apparently excessive concern by a school for those assessments that influence a school's evaluation or the remuneration of the staff, and an apparent lack of concern for other assessments that may mean higher stakes for their children.

The classroom teacher has the responsibility for knowing all of these purposes, for keeping all of them in perspective, and, most of all, for keeping the best interest of the students at heart. Depending on the sources of the tests, there may not be a perfect alignment between the assessment and curriculum and instruction. It is at this point that the purpose of the test must be considered by the teacher. Generally, if assessments have been well selected, and if the students are truly learning, the results will take care of themselves.

Avoid frequent referrals to tests in daily instruction. Avoid telling students they must learn this "because it will be on the test"—rather, provide them with a relevant reason related to their need for this skill or information to accomplish something in the future, and when the time comes for the test, assure them that they have the skills to be successful.

Students deserve to know the purpose of any test they are asked to take. This may be a regular classroom assessment or project, or a state-mandated assessment. They should be told how the results will be used and how their results will affect them. If the test is high stakes for the students, they should be told the consequences of not doing well and what options may be available to them if they do not perform well. When providing students with information about the purpose of a test, teachers should be as reassuring as possible.

Although it is necessary to be honest about a test's purpose, especially in the case where the results will have no impact on the student, it should be made clear to students that they are always expected to do their best. Teachers report that a disturbing trend is developing in schools today whereby students will only put forth effort if an activity "counts" for them in some way. This could be an unintended result of parents rewarding students for report card grades. Some parents actually pay different amounts for the different letter grades their students earn in school. Fewer students seem willing to work because they are intrinsically motivated to do their best. They seem to always expect a reward or payment. However, students who are confident and motivated in the classroom have a difficult time passing up a chance to show what they know, even when it may not count. Creating that kind of atmosphere in the classroom should carry over to the testing situation.

Content

The next important information the teacher must have about state or local assessments is the general areas of content covered. This information is imperative to prepare the students for the test so that the teacher may make accurate interpretations of the test data. Even though a test publisher's test is chosen because it represents most of a system's curriculum, only rarely is there a perfect match.

The following situation is a good example of this phenomenon. An elementary school teacher is going over the content to be covered in the mathematics computation section of a standardized test developed by a test publisher. Although the vast majority of the material to be covered is in the school's curriculum, there are some division objectives for which the students will not have received instruction by the date of the test. This type of division happens to fall in the curriculum for the next school year. What should this teacher do?

This problem is not that unusual, but how it should be addressed depends on the answers to a few questions. First, what is the purpose of the test? Is it high stakes for the students? What will happen if they do not demonstrate these division skills on the test? Second, why is the curriculum covering these objectives in the next grade level?

If the test is high stakes for the students—say, they have to pass it to go on to the next grade—then the curriculum mismatch must be addressed for the sake of the students. In this case, the curriculum must be modified to assure that the students are assessed on material they have learned, or the test must be changed to accommodate the curriculum. Students cannot be penalized because they did not have the opportunity to learn a concept.

It could be that the mathematics content experts for the school system have determined that many students are not developmentally ready for the unit in the current grade level. Therefore, the expectation is that the students would not have learned this material in time for the test anyway (although some of them may.) Let us also assume that this is not a high-stakes test for the students. In this case, it would probably not be in the best interest of the students to adjust the curriculum in this way. This is a time to consult with your principal and perhaps your school district's mathematics leaders to determine the best course of action. Perhaps the decisions will be made to adjust the curriculum. However, it is important to remember that if the curriculum is not adjusted, the students' scores on the mathematics computation test must be interpreted appropriately; the teacher cannot be surprised or defensive that they had not yet learned the division unit.

Sometimes teachers say an assessment does not match their curriculum, but what they mean is that the test does not model the exact way they ask questions in their classroom. For example, teachers will say a question is not worded the way they ask questions in class.

As an illustration, Mrs. Lewis called the district office to complain about the new district assessments she was to administer to her fifth grade class. "It asks the students to provide support for their answer from the text," she says. "My students don't know what 'text' is, so the assessment is not fair! I think you should take the word 'text' out of the test."

It is perfectly reasonable to expect a fifth grader to have been taught the meaning of the word *text*. And the possibility that a district, state, or test company would consider changing the wording of a test question in this case is unlikely. What Mrs. Lewis probably needs to do is teach the word *text* to her students and use the word in her classroom. Obviously, the test designers feel that *text* should be a part of the fifth grade (or earlier) curriculum, and this is probably a reasonable expectation.

In a broader sense, you can help your students be prepared for many different styles of questions when you vary your own way of asking them questions. All teachers have observed their students while taking a test and come away shaking their head, thinking, "They knew that; I know they knew that! Why didn't they just write it down on the test?" Using a variety of words to ask similar questions will strengthen your students' vocabulary and make them more prepared to be able to show what they know regardless of the wording of the question on a test. Always using the same vocabulary to question students has the effect of making them dependent on being asked for the information in exactly that way. Therefore, one minor change that prevents them from accurately interpreting the question can be devastating.

Students should be told the content areas to be covered on an assessment. For standardized tests, they should be given a brief overview of the test sections: for example, there will be mathematics problems to work out, you will be reading and answering questions about the reading, and so on. Students will also benefit from knowing if they might expect to encounter some material on the test they have not been taught. This is more likely when the test to be administered is a national standardized test that does not provide a perfect curriculum match. It could also occur when students are being tested for selection into special programs, and the test may be very challenging. In these cases, students will be less anxious if warned ahead of time that this could occur. They should be encouraged to attempt the items and to do their best, as they may know more than they think.

Periodically, as you read this book, you will encounter *Putting It into Practice*. In these sections you will be given the opportunity to reflect on what you have learned and practice your skills with actual scenarios about students. The purpose of these scenarios is to guide you in evaluating whether student test results actually represent accurate information about students' achievement. After you have read the scenario and formulated your ideas, read through the discussion section, where some possible issues will be discussed.

Putting It into Practice

Scenario One—Fairview

The teachers in Fairview Elementary are excited. Last year, their students didn't do well on the state assessment in mathematics, and they have worked hard all year teaching the students probability and statistics because this was one of the main areas of weakness in the past. The teachers came up with some exciting and challenging activities for the students, and they are sure their students have the skills they need to perform much better on the test this year.

The day of the test arrives, and the test booklets and answer sheets are distributed. As the students work on the test, the teachers walk around the room and observe. Their hearts sink at what they see. The activity their students are working on is similar to many of the activities they completed successfully throughout the school year. But the students are writing "I don't know" or leaving questions blank. As the teachers look more closely at the items, they see that the questions are asking the students if this is a "fair game." This is a term they never used in class, and, apparently, most of their students are not able to generalize from the terms used in class to this new term.

When the scores are reported, the students have not improved their performance from previous years on the probability section of the test. Did the test accurately measure what the students know about probability? Why or why not? How could this situation be avoided in the future?

Discussion

Chances are, if the teachers' assessments during classroom instruction were accurate and on target, these scores are not valid. The teachers had data that indicated that the students had the knowledge to perform well on the test, but the vocabulary used on the test was foreign to them. So although they have the skills they need to perform well, they did not recognize what the test was asking them. Therefore, the unfamiliar vocabulary used in the test becomes a possible explanation for why the students may not have been able to show what they know.

The best way to make sure students will be equipped to recognize what a question is asking is to use many different forms of questioning and a variety of vocabulary words and terms to discuss content. The students themselves may be given an assignment to look up different terms for concepts they are learning about. The less dependent students are on the way a question is asked, the deeper their understanding of a concept will be.

Item Format

A teacher who hopes to do a good job preparing students for a standardized assessment must also be familiar with the format of the items on the test. The strategies students must use to answer different types of items can be quite different, and need to be modeled and taught to students. These strategies can be easily incorporated into regular classroom activities and warm-up activities. The key is to make sure students discuss the ways they make decisions about selected-response items and the ways they approach performance tasks. Modeling by the teacher and *think alouds* will help to introduce these concepts to students. A *think aloud* is an activity whereby a teacher or a student shares the thought process or strategies they are using to solve a problem while processing the problem. Another effective way to teach strategies is to use test taking as an example of when the skill may be useful. For example, a probability lesson in mathematics is a wonderful opportunity to discuss the chances of answering a multiple-choice question correctly if there are four choices and two can be eliminated as incorrect. The most effective way of assuring that students are comfortable with all types of items is to use all types of items in regular classroom assessments. This would include selected-response items (multiple choice, matching, and true or false) as well as constructed response (fill-in-the-blank, brief essay, extended essay, and performance assessment tasks.) Keep in mind that the SAT has essays, constructed response, and multiple-choice items. As of March 2005, SAT test results will consist of three major scores: critical reading, mathematics, and writing. The more variety the students are given, the more prepared they will be for any type of test. And the more variety, the less preparation is necessary before the test. Students who have had previous regular experience with the item types on the test and the strategies necessary to approach them need some brief reminders before the test, not a two-week unit! And those two weeks can more effectively be used for further instruction.

There is a very important by-product of teachers being familiar with a variety of item types and the strategies necessary to respond to each type. Teachers will learn the advantages and disadvantages of each item type, and so they will be able to make better decisions about which to use to assess each skill on their own assessments. And better-quality classroom assessments will result in better instructional decision making!

Students should be told what types of items will be on an assessment test. This kind of information can help students with anxiety about a testing situation, because they often fear the unknown. Knowing what to expect can help them deal with this anxiety, and they can review for themselves the strategies they want to use in studying and responding to test items. For better or worse, it has been suggested that students study differently depending on the type of test items anticipated. D'Ydewalle, Swerts, and De Corte (1983) reported that students told they would be taking an essay exam performed better on a multiple-choice exam than those told they were taking a multiple-choice exam. Apparently, the group expecting the essay exam studied differently.

Putting It into Practice

Scenario Two—Marlyn

Marlyn is a new student in your school from out of state. Only two weeks after she arrives in school, you must administer your district's assessment test in biology. Of course, Marlyn takes the test with everyone else. When the scores are returned to you, you notice that Marlyn has done poorly on the district test. This surprises you, because her grades from her previous school were high, and she does well in class. As you look at her performance in more detail, you note that Marlyn has done well on the multiple-choice section of the test, but she did poorly on the constructed response section.

From this information, do you think Marlyn's test score is valid? Can you think of possible reasons why she did poorly on the district test? What would be your next steps to explore her results further?

Discussion

It is especially important to carefully consider the assessment results of any student who is new to your class. Look at Marlyn's responses on the performance section for clues. Did she answer all aspects of the question or only the initial part? Did she struggle to explain her thinking or how she arrived at her answers? It would be wise to go over the assessment with Marlyn and ask her how she approached the problems. You may find out that Marlyn has never been exposed to performance assessment before, and the format of the test confused her.

Marlyn may need some specific instruction on how to approach this type of assessment. It may be very useful for her and some of the other students in the class to go over the assessment and discuss their answers to the test and how these answers might have been improved. If your observation that Marlyn knows the material is valid, she should only require practice with the assessment format to improve her performance. She should not need further instruction in the biology concepts that were assessed.

Pitfalls to Avoid

Every type of assessment has some pitfalls that certain students are prone to fall into. In this section, we will discuss some of the more common ones for the most common item types. We'll begin with multiple-choice items, because they seem to have more pitfalls and play an important part in standardized and No Child Left Behind assessments.

Common Pitfalls in Selected-Response Testing

In standardized tests with multiple-choice items, students encounter distractors (incorrect answer choices) that would not commonly be used in the classroom. When students encounter these options on a test, the novelty sometimes draws them to make answer choices they would not normally make. This would be a possible source of potential error in the test scores.

Take for example, a multiple-choice test assessing mathematics computation skills. Often, one of the answer choices is "none of the above." This is one of the most typical incorrect answers chosen by students and is particularly a problem for the brightest ones. Why is this such a problem? Does this answer choice pose a threat to score validity?

Classroom assessments in mathematics generally require students to work their own problems or generate their own response. Teachers encourage their students to check their work as they go along. Suddenly, on the test, they are faced with a problem and a set of possible answers. Instead of working the problem, some students find it more compelling to look at the answers and pick one that seems reasonable. Of course, all of the answers represent typical errors made by students. Some students get caught picking one that looks reasonable but is incorrect.

Still, others will use scrap paper to work the problems and then look for their answer in the responses provided. But when students are under time constraints, some of them make computational errors and don't take the time to check their work. Sometimes, in the list of provided answers, they do not find the answer they got when they worked the problem. You can almost see the relief on their faces as they say to themselves, "There is *none of the above!* The correct answer (my answer) isn't here!"

"None of the above" therefore becomes the convenient answer instead of the student having to use the strategies taught to check his or her work. Unfortunately, "none of the above" is rarely the correct response. If students have had previous experience with this option, they are less likely to overuse it during a test. If teachers will give their students the opportunity to develop strategies to select an answer when "none of the above" is an option, it will be a less compelling distractor when the students take a test. Item analyses of your students' responses to these types of items can show you how often this option is chosen by your students. It can also be very revealing to interview them about the strategies they use to choose an answer.

Of course, a test developer will use the "none of the above" distractor on a multiple-choice test because for some students, this incorrect answer is the valid choice. We cannot assume that all students do have the skills we want them to have: thus there is a need for assessments to find out what they know and don't know. Therefore, for the student who does not have the mathematics computation skills being assessed, "none of the above" may be a perfectly acceptable, and valid, response to any given question.

Another distractor commonly used on standardized multiple-choice tests is the option "best as it is" or "correct as it is." These options are typically used in language arts or language mechanics items when students are asked to edit sentence structure, grammar, or punctuation. They are given a sentence, and several different ways of rewriting it. Students who do not read carefully may miss the errors in the sentences and choose the option that the sentence is "best as it is" written. Others who do not have well-developed editing skills (perhaps because they tend to write their own sentences correctly the first time) may correct what their eye sees and never recognize an error. Their tendency will be to choose "best as it is." Practice with these types of questions and answer options will allow students to show what they know on a test instead of getting caught up in compelling and novel answer choices.

Using Scratch Paper

The issue of scratch paper, or scrap paper, is also an important one. Students often believe that using scratch paper is a sign of weakness, indicating they can't "do it in their head." The problem is that in many mathematics computation tests, it is essential to use scratch paper to rewrite the problems. Many are horizontally formatted for a reason. Part of the problem is to be able to align the numbers. For example, look at these two problems:

$$63.7 - 7.3 = \qquad \text{or} \qquad \begin{array}{r} 63.7 \\ -7.3 \\ \hline \end{array}$$

To answer the first problem, the student must know how to align numbers with decimals. To answer the second problem, they do not have to be able to align numbers with decimals, they only need to be able to subtract. Which item do you think would be on the standardized test? If you say the first one, you are right. But students who do the first problem in their head, without rewriting it, are far more likely to make an error. Thus, there is the need to encourage students to use scratch paper to copy and work problems and to learn which problems are important to copy. They must also learn to make sure they copy the problem accurately.

Pacing

Pacing through a test is another possible pitfall. Students need experience with timed assignments before a standardized test. Often, in class they are given sufficient time to finish their work. On a standardized test all students must be given the same amount of time to complete the test (although the allotted time is more than ample for the majority of students, and students with disabilities requiring additional time are given that accommodation). This is the only way scores can be validly compared to the norm group that took the same test. But students without strategies for dealing with time, or who are inexperienced in judging time, can fall behind and not finish the test. For the student whose skills are undeveloped, not finishing the test may be appropriate. But for the rest, not finishing can result in unnecessarily low scores.

So how can teachers make sure students are aware of time? First, give students experience with nonstressful but timed activities. As a general rule, tests allow a little more than one minute per item. Some will take more, some less. Students should be instructed to look ahead to see how many items are on the test so they can pace themselves accordingly. They should also be given experience with what 10 minutes feels like and what 15 minutes feels like so they can judge their progress.

Putting It into Practice

Scenario Three—Tanya

Tanya generally performs quite well in her language arts class. The school system requires that every student take a standardized, norm-referenced test as part of their NCLB assessment. Tanya receives a score of the 35th percentile rank in language arts. When looking over the student results, one of the teachers notices that Tanya did not complete the language arts section of the test (the last 10 items were left blank). Further inquiry reveals that all of the language arts questions that Tanya answered were answered correctly.

Is Tanya's language arts score an accurate representation of what she knows in language arts? What are some issues that should be studied further?

Discussion

The standardized test score is obviously discrepant with other observations and data concerning this student. It was a wise teacher who questioned the results and searched further. What we know about Tanya is that she does have some knowledge of language arts. After all, she did not get one item she responded to wrong! That means there is a possibility that the score of 35 does not represent what Tanya knows, but can we be sure it is not valid?

Remember the purpose of the standardized norm-referenced test—to compare student performance to that of a norm group. So whether Tanya did not know the answers to the last 10 items or is just slow in processing and was not able to finish in a timed situation is actually irrelevant. When compared to the norm group, her score is valid. She only did as well as or better than 35 percent of the norm group. However, if we want to identify a weakness so that it can be addressed instructionally, we will need further information, because it is totally possible that Tanya knows much more than this test indicated. Because Tanya has demonstrated some knowledge, her weakness may be that she cannot pace herself effectively to be able to finish (the problem may be speed, not accuracy). She may be very deliberate and slow to answer each item, or she may have decided to stop when she came to the first item that presented a challenge to her. What we do not know is if Tanya would have answered the last 10 items correctly also had she had the time or confidence to finish the test.

Therefore, some follow-up assessment will be in order, hopefully including a conversation with Tanya about her approach to the test. Students are really the best sources for insights into their needs. Tanya may be able to tell you that she needed more time, and your quick assessments with her may confirm that she does indeed possess the language arts skills assessed, but she did not get to demonstrate them.

Calculator Availability

Some tests are designed with the expectation that students will be allowed to use calculators. The problem is that the test items generally do not require a calculator to solve the problem. So students can get caught up in playing with the calculator and losing valuable time on a test. If students are to be given calculators during testing, be sure they know how and when to use the calculator. There is nothing sadder to watch than a student persistently punching numbers when it is absolutely apparent that he has no idea how to solve the problem using the calculator. All the calculator does is provide help with computation skills and save time spent in computation; it is not a solution to mathematics problems in itself (although as calculator technology advances, some require very little student knowledge to result in a correct answer.)

The use of calculators is a common accommodation made for some special education students. However, the use of a calculator may change what is being assessed by the test. Consider the following example:

$$346 + 77 = ?$$

Without the calculator, a student must be able to write the problem out correctly lining up the digits. The student must know to begin on the right and must be able to add the digits using regrouping. Students must also know their addition facts.

But give students calculators, and they do not have to know any addition facts, they do not need to know how to line up the problem (place value), and they do not need to know regrouping. All that the students with the calculators must know is the order to type in the problem and the proper keystrokes. The calculator has clearly changed what is assessed for one student versus the other, and the student with a calculator has a distinct advantage over the one without it. In a "Legal Corner" article published in the *National Council on Measurement in Education Newsletter*, Phillips (1998) provides a clear analysis of how calculator availability changes the validity of an assessment for a variety of item types and skills assessed.

Constructed Response Pitfalls

Tests requiring students to supply their own answers are called constructed response. On these tests, students are not given a choice of several answers to choose from; they must write out their own answers. This type of test requires a different set of skills that students must know.

First, students must be careful to completely address all aspects of the test questions. Problems may have more than one step, and students will often forget to go back and reread the question after they have written their response to the first section. They must be taught that all sections must be answered.

Second, students are sometimes awarded points based on their approach to a problem or the steps they used to solve the problem. To get those points, they must show all of their work. Many students are reluctant to do this and must be shown that it is in their best interest to do so.

Third, it is important for students to provide adequate evidence to support their answers. It is difficult for young children to believe that the person scoring their answers needs a lot of detail because they obviously are familiar with the content and already know the correct answer! Students can be helped with this problem if they are told to read their answer from the perspective of a fellow student who did not read the original question.

Fourth, students need to be taught self-evaluation skills. They need to construct in their mind, from the clues in the question, what characteristics a good response will contain. Then they need to apply those guidelines when evaluating their own response and be able to edit until the response is a good one. Practice with the class generating and using scoring rubrics can assist students in developing this skill.

Finally, students should be encouraged to look ahead in their performance tasks to see how long the activity is. Attempting every item is important, but some students get bogged down with a confusing item and never get to other items with which they may have more success. Students should be taught to use the number of lines provided for an answer as a cue to how long and detailed the response should be.

Difficulty

Another important piece of information teachers must have about the standardized tests their students will take is the test's relative difficulty. This is an issue particularly essential for correct test score interpretation. The difficulty of the test will in part be determined by the purpose of the test. Take for example three types of tests: a functional-type criterion-referenced test used to certify that students possess some very basic skills, a norm-referenced test, and an advanced placement (AP) exam. The AP exam will be the most challenging by far, followed by the grade level assessment of the norm-referenced test, and then the basic skills test. A high score on the basic skills test would mean much less celebration than the high score on the AP exam. Yet many teachers, not knowing the purpose or level of the tests they administer, cannot adequately interpret and use the results from tests designed for very different levels and for very different purposes. Or they want to know why their students all did so well on the basic skills reading test but were weak on a challenging high school reading assessment. Chances are, those tests assess very different skills, and it is unreasonable to expect similar results, even though they are both referred to as reading tests.

Students deserve to know how challenging they can expect an assessment to be. Obviously, any given assessment may be of a different difficulty level for each student. But students need to be prepared, generally, for what they might expect. This may be especially important if a test is expected to be easy for students, because they need to be encouraged to take their time and respond carefully.

Types of Scores

Test results may be reported in a variety of ways. There are so many possible score types that it is difficult to keep them all straight. Let's take a minute to briefly explore a few of the more common score types. Most standardized tests will use one or more of these score types.

Raw Score

By far the simplest of test scores is the *raw score.* The raw score is the starting point for all other test scores. It is simply a numerical count of the number of items the student answered correctly, or the sum of all of the points awarded to the students' responses. By itself, it has very little meaning unless the score is accompanied by additional information.

For example, brothers Ed and Frank each come home proudly bearing their science test scores. Ed's score is a 10 correct on his eleventh grade test, and Frank's score is a 50 correct on his ninth grade test. What do these scores tell their parents? At first, they might think that Frank has done much better than Ed. But after more closely inspecting the test papers, they find that Ed's test only had 10 items on it, each worth one point each. Frank's test had 25 items on it, each worth three points. So Ed answered everything correctly, and Frank got some items incorrect. What information would have helped the parents come to this conclusion more quickly? It would be a score with more information, such as a percent correct score.

Percent Correct Score

The *percent correct score* would have given the boys' parents additional information. This score is calculated by taking the number correct (or number of points earned) divided by the total number of items on the test (or total possible points), the result multiplied by 100 to convert it to a percentage. So, what would the boys' test scores be when converted to percent correct? Ed's would be $(10/10) \times 100$, or 100 percent. Frank's would be $(50/75) \times 100$, or 67 percent. So now we know that Ed got a larger percentage of possible points on his test than his brother.

But do we know enough to compare scores? Absolutely not. The tests may have had two different purposes. Frank's test may have been much harder. Frank may also have gotten the highest score in his class. So, if we want to know how Frank did in comparison to others, we need still another score. There are several scores that will serve to compare student scores. They are called standard scores, and they all start with a scale score.

Scale Score

A *scale score* is a simple linear transformation of a raw score. (Don't worry about how; test makers publish what is called a *lookup table* to do the transformation—you find the raw score and record the corresponding scale score.) Scale scores are equal interval scores. This means that the distance between any scale score and the next scale score is the same. Therefore, regardless of where the score falls on the scale (top, middle, or bottom), distances between scores are equal and can be compared.

For example, the SAT I is reported as a scale score. We know it as having a mean of 500 and a standard deviation of 100. Anyone with an average score on any version of the SAT I will get a score of approximately 500. The equal interval property means that the difference between a score of 800 and 750 is the same as the distance between a score of 500 and 550, or between 300 and 350. The property of equal intervals also means that scale scores can be manipulated mathematically. They can be summed, averaged, and so on, whereas the standardized scores we will discuss next cannot. Scale scores allow test results from different forms or years of a test to be compared with each other and interpreted. They are often used to make sure a standard remains the same over time. Before we move on to discuss standard scores, we must define the norm group.

Norm Group

For a norm-referenced test, the *norm group* is the group of students used to set the score scales. It will be their scores that determine what score is average, high, or low. Obviously, it is important to know that the norm group is representative of the group whose scores are being compared to it. For example, let's suppose that a test was normed on a group of gifted and talented students from a wealthy California suburb. The test has been administered to a group of average students in an inner city. Is it really useful to see how well these average students stack up against the advantaged students? The group being compared to the norms was not represented in the standardization sample of the test.

Now, this is an extreme example; reputable testing companies go to great lengths to make sure that their norm groups represent as diverse a public as possible to make test scores meaningful for all. This means that the norm groups generally represent the population: if the United States is 50 percent female, the norm group will be 50 percent female; if the United States is 30 percent rural, the norm group will be 30 percent rural; and so on (using ethnic and racial groups and other demographic data).

Percentile Rank

A *percentile rank* describes a student's performance relative to others (generally the rest of a class, or the norm group). On a norm-referenced test, the percentile rank will tell us where the student scored in comparison to the norm group. Percentile ranks range from 1 to 99. By definition, the score tells what percentage of the norm group that the student scored better than. For example, if Stephanie has a percentile rank of 75, it means she scored as well as or better than 75 percent of the norm group. An average score is a 50, meaning the student scored better than half of the norm group, and the other half of the norm group performed better than the student. Percentile ranks can be determined for classroom assessments, too.

A common misinterpretation of a percentile rank is that it is the same as the percentage correct. This, however, is not the case. The two are quite different scores, as we have discussed.

Stanine

The *stanine* stands for standard nine. This is a scale with nine points, three describing scores above average, three at average, and three below average. They are popular because they provide a broader indication of achievement that is easy to understand and does not emphasize small differences between scores. Of course, they are much less precise than the percentile rank score with its 99 possible scores.

Stanines are derived from percentile rank scores. To provide you with an idea of the ranges covered by the stanine scores and the percentile ranks, see Figure 2.1.

Figure 2.1. Stanine Scores Derived from Percentile Rank

Stanine Score	Corresponding Percentile Rank
9	96–99
8	89–95
7	77–88
6	60–76
5	40–59
4	23–39
3	11–22
2	4–10
1	1–3

Notice that the average stanines of 4 to 6 encompass a lot of the scores—from a percentile rank of 23 to 76. This is most of the scores, as we would expect. However, the 4 is a low average, and the 6 is a high average.

Grade Equivalent

The *grade equivalent* is a special type of score because it is the only one that helps us look at performance across grade levels. The grade equivalent score represents the year and month in the continual years of school. A grade equivalent score of 3.6 represents performance typical of a student in the sixth month of third grade.

Grade equivalent scores are by far the most difficult to understand. A grade equivalent of 4.8 means that the student scored the same as a student in the eighth month of fourth grade. If a second grader obtains a grade equivalent of 4.8 on a second grade reading test, it *does not* mean that the student has the skills of a typical student in the eighth month of fourth grade. It means that the student's performance on the *second grade* test is theoretically equivalent to the typical performance of students in the norm group who had completed eight months of grade 4 (and remember, those fourth graders in the norm group took a second grade test, so we expect them to do quite well on it!)

Therefore, grade equivalents cannot be used to place students in grade levels corresponding to their test scores. The second grader with the score of 4.8 should not be placed in a fourth grade reading class as a result of the test score alone. The student took a test designed to measure second grade skills.

The score of 4.8 gives us an indication that the student reads considerably better than the average second grade student. However, it does not tell us if the student has mastered any third or fourth grade level reading skills. In fact, if the student were given a test designed for fourth grade, it is unlikely (though not impossible) that the score would be as high.

Most test publishers recommend against using grade equivalent scores to report results to parents. But you may still run across grade equivalent scores, and now you know how carefully they must be interpreted.

Putting It into Practice

Scenario Four—Bruce

Bruce's parents are thrilled. After their fifth grade son had B's on his report card all year, they just received his standardized test scores, and the report says Bruce's grade equivalent in reading is 7.2. Bruce's parents have high hopes for their son and have been frustrated at the school's reluctance to put Bruce in the gifted and talented (GT) reading class. This reading class works two grade levels above the students' regular grade level. Bruce's parents feel that they finally have the data they need to convince the school to enroll Bruce in GT reading. When they meet with the principal, they proudly share their results and demand that Bruce be put in the GT reading class.

What should the principal tell Bruce's parents? Should Bruce be put in GT reading? How do you know?

Discussion

The principal must explain that Bruce has done very well on his fifth grade reading test, much better than the average fifth grader. But the principal must also explain that there is no information on his sixth or seventh grade skills, because he took a fifth grade test. It would be necessary to give Bruce additional assessments that included the skills he would not be taught if he skipped the sixth grade instructional program in reading. If Bruce performs well on those assessments, it may be time to let him give the GT class a try. But based on the data available right now, the picture is incomplete. It would be wrong to enroll Bruce in GT reading solely on the basis of his grade equivalent score, although he probably does need challenging reading instruction.

Cut Score

The *cut score* is the score on a criterion-referenced test that determines the level of proficiency. For a test that assigns only pass or fail status, there will be one cut score. Students who score at or above the cut score pass, those scoring below the cut score fail. Other tests may use several cut scores, for instance, to classify students as advanced, proficient, or basic. Such a test would have two cut scores, to divide scores into three groups. An example of a 50-point test may look like Figure 2.2.

Figure 2.2. Cut Score Example

Proficiency Level	Cut Score	Score Range
Advanced	47	47–50
Proficient	40	40–46
Basic		1–40

The NCLB legislation requires data on the percentage of students meeting state proficiency standards to determine if adequate yearly progress has been made. Therefore, states are using cut scores similar to these to report the percentage of students scoring in each category. As we approach the 2013–2014 school year, the percentage of students scoring in the proficient and advanced categories must increase, and the percentage scoring in the basic category ultimately must be zero for all students and all subgroups. This is actually a very effective way for teachers to monitor the progress of their students' progress too, because it is easy to implement and explain to parents.

A Word of Caution

A very common mistake is made when teachers desire to complete mathematical computations with student scores, usually to provide some sort of summary. Usually, they wish to average a set of scores. But some of the derived scores, that is, scores that are developed on a given scale, such as the percentiles or stanines, cannot be mathematically manipulated accurately. This is because the intervals between the scores are not necessarily equal. Instead, the scale scores of the students must be averaged, then the corresponding percentile or stanine score must be looked up.

Keep in mind that it is the teacher's responsibility to become familiar with the types of scores used to report their students' assessment results.

Each type of score has particular strengths and weaknesses. Teachers must know what these are to accurately interpret and use results. It is most important for the teacher to be well informed about which of the scores are used to report assessment results.

Students should be taught enough about the types of scores that will be used with their assessments so that the results will be meaningful to them. This is especially important for classroom assessments, but knowledge about scores on standardized tests also would be appropriate for older students.

NCME Code

One important document can serve as a valuable resource to you as you strive to further define your professional development needs in the area of assessment. The NCME Code, (Schmieser et al., 1995) first discussed in the Preface, was adopted "for all individuals who are engaged in educational assessment activities in the hope that these activities will be conducted in a professionally responsible manner . . . . The code is intended to serve an educational function: to inform and remind those involved in educational assessment of their obligations to uphold the integrity of the manner in which assessments are developed, used, evaluated, and marketed." (page 2, Preamble)

Divided into eight sections, the Code defines specific responsibilities for those who

1. Develop assessment products and services (such as classroom teachers)
2. Market and sell assessment products and services
3. Select assessment products and services
4. Administer assessments
5. Score assessments
6. Interpret, use, and communicate assessment results
7. Educate others about assessment
8. Evaluate educational programs and conduct research on assessments

Teachers are intimately involved with the responsibilities in sections one, three, four, five, and six.

You are urged to obtain a complete copy of the Code from NCME.

Summary

Becoming familiar with the assessments your students must take will require some time and effort, but it can result in big payoffs. Demystifying the test for students helps them see their teacher as their coach and mentor. Students who have a caring teacher, one who is seen as believing in them and helpful, report being more engaged and successful in their education. Parents have more confidence in teachers who are knowledgeable about their child's assessments and who can adequately explain test results. The issues covered in this chapter also provide the necessary foundation for the effective use of assessment data in planning appropriate instruction.

You should be prepared to enter into an agreement with your students that you will tell them as much as possible about the assessment they are about to take, whether it is a state-mandated test or a classroom assessment. You should be prepared to tell them the purpose(s) of the test and what information you hope to gain. Avoid telling students that a state or local assessment is not your test, and you will not get any information from it. Your students trust you, and they need to feel that you believe in the value of anything you ask them to do. Learn enough about the test to make sure you can learn something about your students and your instruction.

Tell your students about the content areas to be covered by the test, the format of the items, and whether or not they should guess. Be sure to share any pitfalls they should be aware of and explain how difficult they might expect the test to be. If you expect that there might be items they do not know, tell them that ahead of time, reassure them that it is okay, and encourage them to do their best. Let them know how long they can expect the test to be and whether it is timed or untimed (i.e., they will have all the time they need). Teach them about the scores they will receive.

Once you are convinced that you should know more about the assessments your students take, how can you get the information you need? Every test developed by a reputable test publisher has a variety of manuals for teachers. Make sure that your school has a copy, and if not, request that the principal purchase at least one copy. Similar information about state-developed tests should be available from your State Department of Education if your local school system does not have it. Remember, the more you ask for the information you need to do your job, the more responsive assessment professionals will be. Teachers should never be asked to administer a test for which they have inadequate or incomplete information.

Finally, an important advantage to being familiar with your students' standardized tests is that you should never be surprised at their results. Being informed means that the students will be better prepared, because the teacher will be using similar assessments in the classroom. Therefore, teachers will already know how well their students have learned what is going to be assessed. A very effective staff development tool is to have teachers predict the test results of their classes before they get to see them. Any teacher who says "I have no idea" definitely needs further information about what is assessed, how it is assessed, and the standards used for scoring.

Can we trust the data we get from assessments? Not always. How can we know when the data are accurate? We would not want to make instructional decisions based on faulty data! Teachers must know measurement concepts so that they can evaluate the usefulness of each student's score and determine if the test data can be used to make good instructional decisions.

Chapter 3 deals with measurement concepts. Understanding measurement concepts will go a long way to promote excellence in classroom assessment. Note that we will discuss measurement concepts, not measurement formulas. Please don't be tempted to skip Chapter 3. If you skip it, the rest of the book will not be meaningful to you. It is essential that teachers be able to accurately interpret their students' assessment results to be able to use them effectively to inform their instruction. This is especially relevant now that the NCLB Act requires that all students receive instruction appropriate to their needs. At least give Chapter 3 a chance to help you develop your skills in analyzing test results, both standardized and classroom.

References

D'Ydewalle, G., Swerts, A., & De Corte, E. (1983). Study time and test performance as a function of test expectations. *Contemporary Educational Psychology, 8*(1), 55–67.

Phillips, S. E. (1998). Calculator accommodations. *NCME Quarterly Newsletter, 6*(1), 2.

Schmeiser, C. B., Geisenger, K. F., Johnson-Lewis, S., Roeber, E., and Schafer, W. (1995). *Code of Professional Responsibilities in Educational Measurement*. Washington, DC: National Council on Measurement in Education.

3

Essential Measurement Concepts

All college students can easily recall a course or two they faced with fear. For aspiring teachers, this course is often the one having to do with measurement. Given the importance of this training to the success of a teacher's future, this is a situation that the measurement community must address. A significant part of the problem is that most teacher education programs require only one and possibly two courses on measurement. This is not sufficient for adequate teacher preparation, and as the professors try to cram the needed information into their limited course hours, it becomes overwhelming for many students, especially the ones who approached the experience with fear to begin with. Yet another problem is that too often, in their zeal and enthusiasm for their profession, the measurement specialist will present a lot of technical information and formulas that their students have difficulty translating into real-world applications. A far more reasonable approach would be to incorporate measurement concepts into a variety of education courses.

This discussion is an attempt to present measurement information in a way so that teachers can see how to use it in their classrooms. This chapter is designed to help you see how measurement concepts can help you use your assessment data and make accurate decisions about the future of your instruction. Because some of the information about these concepts is more essential than others, the less essential information is labeled *Digging Deeper,* so that if the going gets tough, you can skip these sections and come back to them when you have become more comfortable with the essential concepts.

Measurement Error

Most of us can remember a test we took that we thought yielded inaccurate results. The results may have been inaccurate for any number of reasons. Perhaps you had a terrible headache on the day of the test and did not do your best, or the test items did not seem to reflect what you had learned in class, or you did not understand what the test items were asking. Of course, this is not an exhaustive list. These are examples of sources of measurement error. Measurement error is an essential concept because it potentially exists in *every* test score. The perfect test is rare. Most of us haven't been exposed to it yet in education. Therefore, each time we assess our students, we are actually getting an estimate of what they know and can do. How good this estimate is will be determined by the amount of measurement error in the score.

Consider the following example. A parent calls the district's testing office in a panic. "I just found out my son can't read!" A patient director of testing ascertains the following information: The parent has just received his son's first norm-referenced, standardized test score. The parent reads a story with his son, Matt, every evening, and they discuss what the story is about. The school reports Matt is making good progress in reading. Every other piece of evidence seems to suggest Matt can read. So why the low test score? When the director of testing calls the school for additional information, Matt's teacher says that he had some difficulty adjusting to his first standardized test experience. He seemed nervous and distracted during the first part of the initial testing session. Because this was the reading part of the test, the teacher is not concerned about the score because she knows Matt can read. Instead, she plans to work with him to help him become more comfortable with a formal assessment situation. Most likely, measurement error interfered with an accurate assessment of Matt's reading ability. But perhaps the most frightening aspect of this scenario is the idea that Matt's parent was willing to ignore all of the other information that existed about his son's progress in reading in favor of this one, limited sample of performance.

In test theory, every score is made up of two independent components: the true score and the random measurement error score. The true score would be the optimum score to have. It could be described as the mean of an infinite number of repeated measurements assuming no changes in motivation or knowledge and/or skill level. But because we cannot obtain a true score, we must be aware that the scores we have include measurement error.

Reliability

We aren't going to discuss any of the different formulas that can be used to determine the reliability of a test score. You can find those in an array of measurement textbooks. Rather, we are going to concentrate on the concept of reliability. Basically, reliability is the consistency of a measurement. If you gave your students an assessment at 10:00 a.m., and repeated it at 11:00 a.m., assuming no change in their motivation and/or knowledge and skill from one administration to the other, and no practice effects, you would expect to get the same results for each student. That is, you assume the test scores are consistent or reliable. However, measurement error on one or both administrations could affect that result.

It is very important to understand that reliability is a property of the score. It is *not* a property of the test. When reliability coefficients (the term used to describe an index of reliability) are reported, they relate to a specific set of test scores (Thompson & Vacha-Haase, 2000). A test score may be reliable in one setting and not reliable in another. That is why it is so important for each teacher to consider the reliability of *each* student's score on each assessment.

As an example, say you use a tape measure attached to a wall to record Fran's height. The same tape measure is used to take each measurement. After five measurements of 4 feet, 10 inches, it is safe to assume that the measurements (scores) are reliable, and Fran is 4 feet, 10 inches tall. Then it is Teri's turn. You use the same tape measure. Measurement number one is 4 feet, 8½ inches. Measurement number two is 4 feet, 9 inches, and measurement number three is 4 feet, 9½ inches. Has Teri grown an inch in less than three minutes? Not likely. Are these reliable scores? No. Have the increments on the tape measure changed? No. All of a sudden, you realize the tape measure has come loose from the wall and is sliding down, slowly. The test (tape measure) stayed the same for both students, but Fran's scores were reliable and Teri's were not. Teri's scores had measurement error (the tape measure coming loose).

We talked about how reliability will be different for each group tested. Let's explore that issue a little further. You administer the same assessment to two different classes (groups). The first group is a rather homogeneous group; that is, they have very similar levels of skill and knowledge on the material being assessed. When you consider the reliability of their test scores, you look at the consistency with which students are ranked on the assessment over multiple administrations. Therefore, for the assessment to be reliable you would expect that, given multiple administrations of this same assessment, the student scores would be ranked in the same order (i.e., Tracey always has the highest score, Cathy always ranks second, Darlene is always at the bottom, etc.) Because the students have very similar knowledge and skills, there will not be much difference between their scores to begin with (the scores are likely to be bunched closely together). What actually happens, however, is that because of measurement error, small changes in a student's score can result in large changes in a student's ranking within the group (because the scores are so close together). This means that the scores are not as reliable as you'd like them to be.

Your second class is much more diverse (heterogeneous) in their knowledge and skills related to the material being assessed. Therefore, their scores are much more spread out. This means that measurement error will have less impact on the reliability of this group's scores. The chance that measurement error will be significant enough to cause a change in a score significant enough to change a student's rank in the group is less likely in this group because the scores are more spread out. This means a one- or two-point change in a score will most likely not change a student's rank in the group. The scores for this group will be more reliable than those for group one. But keep in mind, you used the *same* test. Again, reliability is not a property of the assessment or test. It is a property of the scores!

This example shows that the reliability of the scores will be influenced by the distribution of scores within the group tested (Cunningham, 1986; Guilford & Fruchter, 1978). It will be important for teachers to be familiar with the distribution of their class' test scores, that is, what was the most common score (mode) and what was the middle score (median), how far were the scores from the average, and what were the lowest and highest scores.

Digging Deeper . . .

To make sure you are familiar with the different types of reliability studies typically done by test publishers, we'll mention them here. Each of these types of studies results in a reliability coefficient. Recall our discussion of true score and measurement error. Reliability coefficients give us an indication of the part of the test score variance that is due to the true score, as compared with the part due to measurement error. The reliability coefficient is an index ranging from 0 to 1.0, with 0 indicating no relationship between the two sets of test scores and 1.0 indicating a perfect relationship. Obviously, the higher the reliability coefficient, the more reliable the scores.

A *test-retest* study is the type we have been using in our examples thus far. In short, a test is administered multiple times (usually twice) to a single group. Reliable test scores will result in the same rank-ordering of individuals for each administration. The problem with actually conducting a test-retest reliability study is that it is impossible to administer the same test multiple times without the scores changing because of practice effects, changes in motivation, and so on. Therefore, this type of reliability study, although good for conceptual understanding, is not particularly practical.

An *internal consistency* reliability study (or *split-half*) can be accomplished with one test administration. The test is then divided into many sets of pairs of items, considered to be alternate forms of each other. *Alternate forms* are tests measuring the same thing, with different items. In this case, we are assuming that each item measures the same thing, and therefore the correctness of the response to one item should be strongly related to the correctness of the response to the second item. Individuals' scores on the item pairs are compared. Reliability is estimated from the average of the relationship between the responses to the pairs of items. This is the most practical study to conduct, but it does have its limitations. The most important limitation is that the longer a test is (the more items it has), the more reliable the scores. Therefore, cutting a test in half will almost surely reduce the reliability of the scores and underestimate the reliability of the scores of the entire test. There are statistical procedures to predict total test score reliability from these data, however.

In a *parallel forms* study, students take two forms of a test that have been designed as parallel, alternate, or equivalent. The tests are designed to assess the same skills and have the same degree of difficulty, yet they use different items. For example, there are many different items that could be used to assess a student's ability to compute using the multiplication algorithm, because we can easily change the numbers we ask them to multiply. If we divide these items into two equally challenging tests, we have two parallel forms. Parallel forms are often used to conduct a pre- and post-test of students' skills, sort of a before and after instruction assessment.

When parallel forms of a test are used to establish reliability, we must assume there are no changes in the examinees between the test administrations. The scores for each individual should be the same on both tests, if the scores are reliable.

Some Factors Affecting Reliability

Test Length

In the discussion of internal consistency reliability studies, test length was mentioned as a factor influencing reliability. It has long been known that one way to increase the reliability of the scores is to lengthen the test. This makes some sense, in that a longer test samples more behaviors. It also means that each item has less impact on the score than items on a shorter test.

When interpreting scores from a typical standardized test, it is common to have scores from two or more subtests, such as mathematics concepts and mathematics computation, and a total mathematics score that combines the two. The total mathematics score will be the most reliable, because it is based on the items from the two subtests. The combination will also result in a longer test.

This is a very important concept because with the inclusion of more constructed-response items (essays, performance tasks, etc.) on tests, the number of items has been reduced. This means that tests including items that may take longer for students to respond to will, by definition, be less reliable than previously used tests that included more items. Research has shown that these "new kinds of items are, in a sense, only half as reliable as the old" (Wainer, 1996).

Digging Deeper...

Group Composition

As discussed earlier, the composition of the group being assessed will affect the reliability of the test scores. The scores for a very homogeneous group (relative to the skills or knowledge being assessed) will be less reliable than those of a very diverse, or heterogeneous group.

Local Independence

The term *local independence* refers to the independence of the test items. If items are independent, it means that the answer to one item is not dependent, or influenced by, the answer on another. As the examinee approaches each item, his or her performance on the previous item(s) is irrelevant. However, in many performance assessments, students are paced through a scenario that builds on previous performance. Whether or not they get item eight correct may well depend on whether they got item six and/or seven correct. Even in the case where the items don't depend on each other, they may all refer to a single reading passage or other stimulus, meaning the items are dependent measures (Yen, 1993). If the items are not locally independent (that is, they depend on each other, or are related) the reliability of the scores will be reduced because in effect the test is actually shorter than it would appear, given the total number of items.

Wainer (1996) conducted a study of the reliability of the new SAT reading comprehension test. This new version makes use of several long reading passages, followed by an average of 10 items. By definition, these 10 items are dependent on each other, therefore their reliability is reduced. Wainer found that the test length would need to be almost doubled to regain the reliability lost because of dependent items. The bottom line for teachers is to remember that as item types that are related to each other (such as performance assessments, and other constructed response or dependent items) are added to student tests, score reliability will be reduced, even though testing time may be extended. In other words, test length is an issue relating to the number of independent test items, not merely a count of the responses required on the test. Just because a test takes longer for students to complete does not mean the test scores are likely to be more reliable.

Interrater Reliability

Before we wrap up our section on reliability, we must discuss one more type of reliability of importance to the teacher. *Interrater reliability* has become more of an important issue because the resurgence of constructed response items (essays, extended responses, brief responses, etc.) These are test items that require the student to construct a response to the question; they do not select from possible answers provided to them. This means that each student is providing a different response, which must be scored in a fair and unbiased way. To do this, a scoring guide or rubric is required to guide the scorer. A problem with this type of item, most often brought up by parents, is the perceived subjectivity of the scoring.

One way to address this issue is to look at interrater reliability. Remember that reliability is the consistency of the score. In this case, we need for the student's response to get the same score regardless of which teacher scores it (between-rater reliability) and regardless of when it is scored (within raters over time). This is a simple kind of study for teachers to do because they need only to have several of them score the same papers and compare the scores. If they all assign the same score to a given response, the score is reliable. If the scoring varies, the score is not reliable.

Of course there can be several reasons for variance between the scores. If the scoring guide or rubric is insufficient, it will allow for subjective interpretation, which will vary among teachers. Also, teachers may have different understandings of what the standard is, that is, what the definition of each score point is. This can happen even if the scoring guide is sufficient, because some teachers will not refer to it as closely as others. This is when students will begin to say that one teacher scores "harder" than another.

Interrater reliability is an important reliability concept because it contributes to the ability of the teacher to fairly compare student scores. Given the teacher's limited time, perhaps the most effective way to achieve and maintain interrater reliability, at least among the teachers in your grade level, course, or school, would be to grade a sample of papers and then trade them around. After each teacher scores a few papers, share the scores and discuss any discrepancies. Just the process of coming to a consensus on a few papers can help everyone to define and internalize standards.

Putting It into Practice

Scenario Five—Berkley High

The ninth grade English teachers at Berkley High are in a quandary. They have just compiled their data from their first grade-wide assessment of the school year. The assessment requires each student to write two brief essays and one extended essay based on topics from a novel they have read. Each teacher has completed a chart for each class that shows how many of his or her students scored at various levels on the English assessment. The chart shows how many students scored above proficiency, at proficiency, and below proficiency.

The confusion arises from the fact that Mrs. Ellison's honors class has a small number of students above proficiency, and Mr. Hamilton's remedial class has a large number of students at proficiency. The teachers expected Mrs. Ellison's class to have more students above proficiency (because they are advanced students) and Mr. Hamilton's class to fewer students at proficiency (because they are struggling). The remaining teachers had results more in line with the team's expectations.

What are possible explanations for the discrepancy the teachers found? What other information should they consider?

Discussion

This could be an example of inadequate interrater reliability. The teachers had expectations for the students' performance, but they may not have all been using the same standard to score the assessment. Mrs. Ellison is used to seeing responses from students who perform very well, and she may have a tendency to be tough on her students. Mr. Hamilton, however, has the opposite situation. He may reward what he sees as progress in his students' performance with a grade representing proficiency, when the student has not actually demonstrated proficiency. The key to the quandary may be to have Mrs. Ellison, Mr. Hamilton, and the other teachers sit down and regrade the papers from these two classes. Before they start grading, it would be important for all of them to review the criteria for an above proficiency, at proficiency, and below proficiency response. As they grade the papers, the teachers should compare the scores each of them assigned to each paper and discuss their reasons for the score. As they work together, they will come to an agreement and understanding about the criteria they are using and will gain valuable practice using that criteria.

Mrs. Ellison may realize that many of her students perform well above the definition of proficiency, but that definition is a little lower than she thought. In fact, the scale for the assessment may not even accommodate the high level of performance her students demonstrate. Mr. Hamilton may gain a new understanding of just what proficiency is and realize that his students have some progress to make before they get there.

This activity is important because when schools want to compare the performance of many students, the standards or criteria used to grade all of those students must be the same. This is the only way valid comparisons can be made. It may also make it clear to the teachers how important it is that the students are aware of the criteria used to assess the students' work.

Reliability is a complex subject, and this short introduction to the concept does not do justice to the excellent and comprehensive body of literature that exists. However, it is unrealistic to expect all teachers to embrace the challenge of joining the discussion of the measurement community. Although it is hoped that some teachers will be encouraged to do so, it is also hoped that the rest have a basic understanding that will serve them in their classroom. We will apply these concepts to the interpretation and use of student data in Chapters 5 and 6.

In the meantime, congratulations on making it this far! If you have a general concept of what reliability is and some of the issues you need to be aware of to maximize reliability of student scores, the section was a success. If you are now willing to consider the question "If I administered this test again today, am I quite confident I'd get the same results?" for each of your students, then you are beginning to understand measurement concepts. Let's continue building those skills.

Standard Error of Measurement

Statistical estimates of reliability (reliability coefficients) do not relate to the score for an individual student. They always relate to a group. So how do we get an estimate of how much measurement error we have in each individual student's test score? We use the *standard error of measurement.* The standard error of measurement is computed from the reliability coefficient, but it is not dependent on the variability of the group tested. It is like a standard deviation from a student's true score. Although we can never know a student's true score, as discussed earlier, each measurement is an approximation. If we were able to take many measurements of the same student, the test scores would cluster around the true score. If the test scores were very reliable, the scores would be close to the true score. If the scores were not reliable, they would fall away from the true score.

So how can we use a standard error of measurement? The best way to use a standard error of measurement is to assume that the student's actual score is the true score. Add the value of the standard error of measurement to the score and subtract the standard error of measurement from the score. This gives you a range that probably includes the student's true score.

Upper range: Score + Standard error of measurement

Lower range: Score – Standard error of measurement

Let's try an example. Portia has a score of 85 on the XYZ test. The standard error of measurement is 2.5. We add 2.5 to 85 and get 87.5. We subtract 2.5 from 85 and get 82.5. Portia's true score is probably between 82.5 and 87.5. If we want to be even more sure we have an accurate range of estimates for the true score, we could take two times the standard error of measurement and do our plus and minus. Then Portia's true score would fall between 80 and 90, a wider range, but one almost sure to include her true score.

If we assume that the scores on the XYZ test are percentage correct scores, we know that a score of between 80 percent and 90 percent is probably quite good. But let's say Zachary's score is 52. The standard error of measurement for a score of 52 will most likely be different from the standard error of measurement for a score of 85. This is because tests are designed for different purposes, and information may be more accurate at some points on the scale than others. For example, a test to determine mastery of a skill will be designed to be most accurate (and provide the most information) at the score point where mastery is determined. In the case of the XYZ test, if a student must score at least 85 percent to be classified as a "master" of the skill assessed, the scores right around 85 percent will be the most accurate (have the smallest standard error). It is not as important to distinguish as accurately between students scoring 30 percent or 35 percent correct because they aren't close to the standard and neither one of them will be classified as masters.

Remember Zachary's score of 52? If the standard error of measurement for the score of 52 is 5, and we want to double it to make sure we've included his true score in the range, his true score would be between 42 and 62. This is a much wider range than Portia's, so we know that Zachary's score could be less accurate than hers.

Now say that for the ABC test, the standard error of measurement for Zachary is 2. Does this mean that the XYZ test scores are less reliable than the ABC test scores? Not necessarily. The standard error of measurement is based on score points, and tests often have different score scales. To *compare* the reliability of test scores, the reliability coefficients should be used.

Although you will not always have access to the standard error of measurement for your student's standardized test scores, understanding the concepts helps to remind you that the scores are not a picture of the student's brain but an estimate. And if a standard error of estimate is available to you, then you will know how to use it. The concept can be especially useful when looking at group scores over time, because the standard error of measurement can help you to determine if changes in scores are due to real progress, or just due to fluctuation.

Validity

Validity is the most important test score characteristic for the teacher. Validity asks the questions "Does the test assess what it was designed to assess?" and "Did I get the information I intended to get?" Like reliability, validity is not a property of the test, validity is a property of the test score interpretation (Popham, 1997). Most important, a test score interpretation may be valid for one student in the class and not at all valid for the second.

The relationship between reliability and validity is an important one. An assessment can't possibly measure what it was intended to measure if it results in a different score on every administration. A test or assessment that is not reliable cannot be valid. So, reliability is a necessary but not sufficient requirement for validity.

The goal is to make assessment data as valid as possible so that we can use the data to plan instruction for the students. Teachers who are familiar with the concepts of validity are better able to evaluate their students' assessment data and make valid instructional decisions. Validity is *the key* to the appropriate interpretation of assessment data and to its usefulness in informing instruction to meet student needs.

Putting It into Practice

Scenario Six—Yuri

Yuri just arrived in the United States one month ago. He and his family speak very little English. His teacher wants to assess Yuri's math skills so she can place him in the appropriate instructional group. The assessment the teacher gives Yuri includes many word problems and involves some reading. Yuri does very poorly on the math assessment, and the teacher places him in a below-grade-level group. Less than one year later, to everyone's surprise, Yuri achieves a very high score on a very challenging math test, given to students as one criterion for selection into the gifted and talented math program.

Was the initial evaluation of Yuri's math skills valid? That is, did it accurately represent his math skills? Can you think of reasons why the assessment results may not have been valid?

Discussion

Unfortunately in education, this type of situation happens too often. Teachers need to have the freedom and knowledge to select and administer appropriate assessments. Most likely, Yuri's low assessment results were a result of his inability to read or understand the English language. Therefore, the assessment did not assess his math skills, it became yet another assessment of his English skills, which we already knew were weak. So the interpretation of the mathematics assessment results for Yuri was invalid. In fact, the assessment was inappropriate for him.

In order for a teacher to make sound decisions based on student assessment results, the teacher must be willing to consider possible threats to the validity of the test score. If there is a chance that one of these threats existed (as it did in Yuri's case), then the only alternative is to assess the student in some different ways, making sure the alternative assessments do not have similar validity threats. Remember that the No Child Left Behind (NCLB) assessments must be administered to 95 percent of all students and student groups. In some cases, these assessments may be inappropriate for the students, and teachers will not always have the ability to substitute a more appropriate test. In these cases, test results must be interpreted and used with extra care so that students are not provided with unnecessary or inappropriate instruction based on invalid test results.

Types of Validity

There are several types of validity discussed in measurement literature. Teachers should be familiar with all of these types to consider any possible threats to the validity of their interpretation of student scores. Let's start with content validity.

Content Validity

This is one of the easiest types of validity to consider, because it is generally based on an expert's opinion and does not require a research study. Also referred to as *face validity*, *content validity* addresses the issue of representativeness and coverage. For example, if you look at the items on the test, does it appear that the items measure the curriculum, and are the items an adequate sample of that curriculum? When students complain that a test focused on an obscure area of the content, they are complaining about content validity. If you take a test that you felt you were prepared for, but find that the questions you anticipated were not included, but the ones that were not emphasized in class or in the supporting materials were included, you are questioning the test's content validity.

Digging Deeper...

Construct Validity

Construct validity is the extent to which a test measures a trait. It deals with the idea of whether what is being measured is distinct, meaningful, and related to other concepts in a logical way. Therefore, much of construct validity is dependent on data that provides information about the trait the test purports to measure. Often, construct validity is established by studying a test's relationship to other tests, or how the test scores change because of experimental manipulation of related variables.

For example, if a test is designed to assess persistence, one would not expect the resulting test scores to correlate with the scores from a test assessing math ability. The correlation of the persistence test and a second measure of persistence is expected to be high, however. If both of these expectations were confirmed, we have evidence of construct validity.

If children were administered the persistence test, then given encouragement and experience in persistence, and then given the test again, one would expect the persistence scores to go up, that is, to be influenced by training in persistence. If the scores did go up, we would have additional evidence of construct validity. Construct validity is built as these pieces of consistent information are assembled.

Criterion Validity

A test score interpretation has *criterion validity* if the test yields similar results as other assessments, which were designed to measure the same thing (a criterion). In other words, we would expect a student to be classified similarly given two separate and distinct measures of the same thing. For example, the gifted and talented program uses Test A to select students for participation. This test has been used for years, and 98 percent of the students selected using the test have been successful in the program. The program would like to adopt Test B because it is shorter and easier to score. Test A is the criterion test, and to establish criterion validity, Test B must result in the same students being selected for the program as were selected by Test A.

Consequential Validity

The measurement community is in a state of controversy over a proposed new type of validity referred to as *consequential validity*. Messick (1989) argues that not only does a score interpretation need to be valid, but any implications for actions taken based on this interpretation need to be valid as well.

He argues that responsibility for this validity research rests with test publishers and measurement experts. On the other hand, Shepard (1997) presents the argument that the validation of a test score interpretation for a specific use (consequence) is the responsibility of the test user. This is a very simplified summary of a complex debate, but the importance for teachers is that they must be cognizant of the potential misuse of test score interpretations for decision making.

Let's go back to Yuri, for example. The consequence of Yuri's teacher's interpretation of his test score was that Yuri was placed in a low-math-skills class, when his real weakness was his English skills. This is a consequential validity problem.

Correlations

Correlations are not limited to measurement research. Correlations are statistics used in many different venues. The reason they are included in this chapter is because correlations are very frequently misused and misinterpreted in education. Validity coefficients and reliability coefficients are correlations. Correlations demonstrate that a relationship exists between two variables and provides an indication of the strength of that relationship. Correlations range from negative one (–1, a perfect negative relationship between the variables) to positive one (+1, a perfect positive relationship between the variables). A correlation of zero means there is no relationship between the two variables. The limitation is that a relationship between two variables does *not* mean that one causes the other.

Let's use a classic example. A correlation is found between men's height and weight. It is a positive relationship (.85), meaning as height increases, weight increases. It does not necessarily mean that being tall causes men to weigh more, or being short causes men to weigh less.

Several years ago, insurance company statisticians found a correlation between the number of accidents and the color of the car. Specifically, a high correlation was found between having a green car and being involved in an accident. A misinterpretation of this correlation would be that people who own green cars cause more accidents, or if you have a green car, you are a bad driver. Therefore, the insurance company would charge you higher rates if you drive a green car.

The caution for the reader is to realize that correlation does not imply causation. Just because variables are related does not mean one causes the other. Do not set expectations for students based on correlations, and do not label students based on one variable that is correlated with another.

Limitations of Assessment Data

Our discussion of correlations leads us into a study of a few factors that place limitations on the use of assessment data. Some teachers seem to put too much faith into their assessment results, others may seem to take the results with a grain of salt. Somewhere in the middle is where we need to begin, and after evaluating the situation, we may need to move to one direction or the other, depending on the assessment and the situation.

Means and Standard Deviations

Often, groups of student test scores are reported as means, or averages. To get the average score, the student scores are added up and the total is divided by the number of students in the group. But means can be very misleading under certain circumstances.

Let's look at a few examples. Take a minute to study these two sets of test scores in Figure 3.1. The highest number of possible points on this test is 10. Look at how the distributions of student scores are different, and how they are alike. Which one will have the higher mean? Why?

Figure 3.1. Sample Test Scores from Two Classes: Example 1

Student	Class A	Class B
A	9	9
B	10	3
C	8	8
D	8	8
E	9	9
F	10	10
G	7	7
H	8	8
I	9	9
J	7	7

Hopefully, you noticed that only one score in the two sets of scores is different. Student B in Class A had a 10, Student B in Class B had a 3. Other than that, the scores are identical. How much did that little change in scores affect the mean or average of the class? Well, the average for Class A was 8.5 and the average for Class B was 7.8. This represents quite a difference given that nine of the 10 scores were identical. The entire difference is due to the high score in Class A and that one low score in Class B. With small numbers of students, one outlier score, the one that is very different, can have quite an effect on the mean.

Let's look at another set of test scores in Figure 3.2.

Figure 3.2. Sample Test Scores from Two Classes: Example 2

Student	Class A	Class B
A	10	5
B	10	6
C	9	5
D	10	7
E	9	4
F	2	6
G	1	5
H	2	7
I	3	5
J	1	6

This set of scores is different from those in Figure 3.1. You may have noticed that the first five students in Class A have very high scores, whereas the last five have very low scores. There are no scores in the middle of the score range. In looking at Class B, there are no high or low scores; all of the scores are clustered around the middle. The interesting thing about these two sets of scores is that their means are almost equal. Class A has a mean score of 5.7, and Class B has a mean score of 5.6. So if all we had were the mean scores for these two classes, we'd think they were pretty much alike. But that is not the case at all. Exactly how could we best describe how the scores are different? Class A seems to be made up of two subgroups: high achievers and low achievers. Because the scores vary widely, we would refer to them as heterogeneous. Class B seems to be made up of students who score in the middle range. Because they are all scored alike, they are a more homogeneous group.

To help us tell the difference between these two groups, we would need to have the standard deviation. This is a measure of the dispersion of the scores—how far away is the typical score from the mean score? The larger the standard deviation, the farther the scores are from the mean. So which of the sets of class data would have the largest standard deviation? It would be Class A.

Although teachers may calculate their class's average scores on some assessments, they are much less likely to calculate the standard deviation. But they can still be aware of the spread of the scores by looking at the individual scores. And teachers or school staff receiving only average or mean scores on standardized tests should remember the limitations of that information, and avoid drawing too many conclusions without additional information.

Another limitation of using mean scores is accentuated now that NCLB has emphasized our focus on individual students. Means can have the impact of hiding or deemphasizing the scores of individual students. Average or mean scores can be high, but that mean does not necessarily describe the performance of every student. We need other ways to describe our results that are sure to include every student in a meaningful way. One additional and useful piece of information is the median.

Median

The median is the score that divides a distribution of scores in half. Half of the students score above the median, and half of them score below. Say that a third grade has a median score of the 75th percentile on a norm-referenced reading test. This means that half of the students had scores above the 75th percentile. On a norm-referenced test, given to a normal distribution of students, the expectation would be that half of the students score above the 50th percentile. So this third grade performed considerably better than expected.

Reporting percentages of students scoring in various score ranges helps to make the performance all students visible in the data. If the percentage of students scoring below the 25th percentile (or below proficiency, or a cut score, or any score of interest) is reported, those low-achieving students are not hidden in a mean. The fact that a school has only 5 percent of its students scoring that low, whereas another has 35 percent of their students scoring in that range is very important information when planning for the needs of schools and students to meet the requirements of NCLB and adequate yearly progress (AYP). Reporting percentages of students in categories is also language consistent with reporting the percentages of students meeting state proficiency standards. Teachers can look at percentages of students meeting any number of criteria to help them determine instructional groupings. An important and crucial next step is to identify the individual students in any given group. An instructional plan to meet the needs of each student is fundamental to leaving no child behind.

Test Length

In the discussion on test reliability, we learned that the more independent items that are on a test, the more reliable the test is likely to be. This also means that tests with fewer items will not be as reliable as we might like. Does that mean that we should avoid item types that take students more time to respond to in favor of items students can answer quickly? Absolutely not. Teachers must feel free to choose an appropriate type of assessment for each skill they need to assess. Caution must be used when interpreting the information they get from these shorter tests, realizing that each test is just a sample of a much larger domain of possible test items. Bob, Adrianna, Danny, and Scott may have performed differently if a different sample of test items had been chosen. The best way to make accurate decisions about student learning is to use multiple indicators of their performance (projects, homework, test scores, class demonstration of understanding, etc.).

Age of Students

If you take some time to study the technical manuals of standardized tests, you will notice that test reliability estimates are lower for tests at the kindergarten and first and second grade level than for tests designed for students in grades three and above. This is because students at these ages are very likely to be developmentally in different places, and a norm-referenced test may not be able to adequately capture achievement. Katz (1997) reported that young children are poor test takers because they can be confused by the testing process. They may have difficulty answering a question that they think the examiner must know the answer to.

Even the most child-friendly version of a standardized test will not be reliable and valid for every student. For this reason, it is important not to overinterpret standardized test scores and to use them instead in conjunction with other assessments to evaluate student progress. This is especially important for young children taking their first standardized test. Unfortunately, it is especially difficult to convince parents that they must not overinterpret this first piece of official information! It is your job to try.

Putting It into Practice

Scenario Seven—Ian

Ian is a first grader in your class. Your school uses a standardized test as one indicator to monitor progress in reading skills. Ian's parents are very involved in his education and read to him at home. Although Ian has been making good progress in his reading, he receives an average score in reading on the standardized test. His parents are concerned and make an appointment to see you about Ian's test score.

What will you say to Ian's parents? Do you think Ian's score is valid? Why or why not?

Discussion

Teachers of very young children must always keep in mind the reduced reliability of standardized test scores for young children. If this is Ian's first standardized test (and hopefully it is, because first grade is very early to assess students this way), chances are the results are not as reliable and valid as they should be. Some students suffer from extreme anxiety concerning their first big test, and others just do not have the concentration and test-taking skills to allow them to show what they know. Unless you actually observed Ian closely during the test, you may not be able to comment on how he reacted during testing.

It is important that Ian's parents understand that the standardized test score is just one indicator of Ian's reading skills, and it must be considered in light of the other information available. If Ian is able to demonstrate above-average reading skills in the classroom and at home, chances are his standardized test score does not adequately represent what he knows. However, it may be that Ian is an average reader for his age, and his test score is valid. An understanding and well-informed teacher can help to assure that Ian and his parents are not traumatized by the first standardized test. Refusing to come to final conclusions and use of additional data can reassure parents that he will not be permanently labeled based on his performance on this single test.

Test Bias and Item Bias

As more and more schools boast of their diverse student bodies, more attention must be devoted to potential bias in assessments. Bias is present when the scores of any subgroups are differentially valid. For example, a test biased against Asian students would yield scores for others that were interpreted validly and scores for Asian students that were not valid (did not represent what they knew).

We must make an important distinction here. Bias is only a source of measurement error when the subgroups in question are actually equivalent on the material being assessed. The source of the score difference is therefore due to bias inherent in the measurement instrument. Therefore, if girls in the class really are better writers than the boys, then differential test scores are valid and do not represent bias. The problem is that it is difficult to know when bias really is present.

Standardized test publishers spend much effort and resources to attempt to assure that their tests are as free from bias as possible. Prior to items being included on a test form, they are reviewed by teams of people who look for possible sources of bias against any gender or cultural group. Once the test forms are field tested, they have sophisticated (although not perfect) methods to detect what is termed *differential item functioning* (DIF). They use statistical methods to determine which items are functioning differently for members of different subgroups. Items with statistically significant evidence of DIF are removed from the assessment. However, some studies have shown that tests may not be fair, even after these procedures have been followed.

Langenfeld (1997) conducted a study of gender issues in college admissions tests and found that women score lower on tests with self-selected samples (such as the SAT, where students are not required to participate in testing but may opt to do so). And although women score lower on these tests, they earn higher grades in high school and college. Langenfeld encourages studies using outside criteria to study the potential bias of tests to be added to the current methods to study test bias or differential item functioning.

Lane, Wang, and Magone (1996) did a study of gender differences on mathematics performance tasks. The results were mixed in that some tasks were biased toward females, and some were biased toward males. Some of the factors accounting for bias and which groups they favored were: When the task had a figure, and/or involved geometry, it favored males; tasks that required an explanation of the problem-solving strategy or thought process, and in which students had to show their work, favored females; and tasks set in a real-world context favored males. This study provides teachers with some guidelines about the types of items that may favor males and females.

Teachers must evaluate their own tests by reviewing items for potential bias. They must be willing to learn enough about each student to be able to consider issues of fairness, especially when decisions will be made based on assessment results. One way to do this is to repeatedly talk to the students individually about the questions and how they interpreted them. Another is to closely monitor the types of items students seem to do well with and the types they do not.

Putting It into Practice

Scenario Eight—A Trip to the Art Museum

Your sixth grade class is preparing for a trip to the art museum. You found a performance task that will allow you to assess their writing skills while they plan for the trip. After the writing scores are recorded, you notice that some of your students received unusually low scores. When you look more closely, you realize that most of them are your economically disadvantaged students. The writing topic asked the students to write about what they hoped to see at the museum and how they planned to spend their day there. When you look at the students' responses, you notice that they are very short and undeveloped, yet you know that several of these students are good writers.

Are the scores valid for the economically disadvantaged students? What could have happened and how could you find out more?

Discussion

There is a chance that this writing topic may be biased against disadvantaged students. It assumes some previous experience with art museums that the students may not have had. Therefore, when asked to write about what they hoped to see and how they planned to spend their day, they had insufficient material to write about. The more advantaged students in the class may have already been to an art museum, have a book at home about an art museum, or heard others talking about art museums. It would be helpful if you discussed the assignment with the students, and if they confirm your suspicions, you should assess your students' writing skills with a topic that all students have sufficient background to show what they know. Another option would be a preassessment lesson where all students were given information about art museums, perhaps with a video tour, prior to being asked to write about a visit to an art museum.

Item and Test Difficulty

Two main types of statistics can be generated for test items: item difficulty and item discrimination. *Item difficulty* is based on the number of students answering an item correctly divided by the total number of students answering the item. For instance, if half of the students in a testing group answer an item correctly, the item difficulty is .50. If all of the students answer the item correctly, the item difficulty is 1.0. The more difficult the item, the less likely a large percentage of students will answer it correctly, and the lower the item difficulty statistic will be. An easy item receives a high item difficulty; a difficult item receives a low item difficulty. Item difficulty indices range from 0 to 1.0.

Item discrimination is related to item difficulty because it is an indicator of how well the item discriminates between students who know the material and students who don't. Item discrimination is determined using students' total test scores as an indicator of their competence with the material being assessed. In other words, in general, high-scoring students would be expected to answer items correctly, and low-scoring students would be expected to answer items incorrectly. When all of the low-scoring students answer an item correctly, and the high-scoring students answer it incorrectly, the item did not function as expected. Obviously, an item with an item difficulty of 1.0 does not distinguish between students at all, because everyone answers it correctly (i.e., it is an easy item). An item with a difficulty of 0 does not discriminate between students either, because it is so difficult everyone answers it incorrectly. Maximum discrimination can occur when the item difficulty is approximately 0.50. This is because theoretically, if half of the students answer an item incorrectly, you have the best chance that those students are the ones who don't know the material being assessed. This is the case only if the item is also an effective discriminator.

The concepts of item difficulty and item discrimination can be very helpful to teachers analyzing their own tests. Looking at how many students answered test items correctly and which students answered incorrectly can provide good information about test item quality and potential validity. If the students who seemed to follow the instructions well, answered questions accurately along the way, and generally performed well get a few test items incorrect, chances are there could be something wrong with those test items, and the information available from the test may be flawed. If every student gets a given item incorrect, this may also indicate a problem (either with the test or with the instruction).

Test difficulty is also an important concept. In the case of standardized tests, test difficulty ranges from very basic (easy), as in the case of tests assessing more functional levels of skills, to very challenging (difficult) as in the case of advanced placement exams or other competitive tests. The purpose of the test will determine the distribution of item difficulty for the items making up the test. Take, for example, a norm-referenced test. The purpose of this test is to spread students out on a normal curve, to distinguish between student achievement. The expectation is that most students will be scoring around the 50th percentile (average). Therefore, the majority of test items are of average difficulty. The test will have fewer very easy items and fewer very difficult items because fewer students are expected to score in the very low and very high ranges of the scale.

Similarly, criterion-referenced tests are used to certify that students have met a standard or specified level of mastery. These tests have a cut score—a score that determines whether or not the standard or criterion has been met. Because important decisions will be made based on a student's score, the score must be accurate. One way to make sure of this is to have the majority of items at the difficulty level required by the cut score. This will mean the scores at the cut score will have the least amount of error. Higher error is acceptable at the high ranges of the scores because the purpose of the test is to determine pass or fail. Once a student has passed, further information about the level of mastery is not required. The same goes for the student who does not approach the cut score. The purpose of the test was to determine if the student met the standard; a student who does not approach the cut score has not met the standard.

Knowing the purpose of a test, the approximate difficulty level, and the type of discrimination among students that is required will help the teacher do a better job preparing students for the test and interpreting resulting test scores.

Digging Deeper...

Item Response Theory

When people encounter tests that are high stakes, given year after year to groups of students, they often wonder how the test developer can guarantee that the difficulty of each version of the test remains the same. In other words, how can we be sure that the group taking the test in 2004 is being held to the same standard (no more, no less) than the group that took it in 2000?

The statistical process used to do this is called *equating*, and it can be accomplished in several ways, all fairly technical. The most common way is to use item response theory. A very simplified explanation of the relevant aspect of this theory is that the probability of any given student answering any given item correctly is dependent on several factors. One is the student's ability level. The others are characteristics of the test items: Difficulty and discrimination are the most commonly used. The premise of the theory is that we would expect a student of high ability to answer easy items correctly with a high probability, and we would expect low ability students to answer difficult items with a very low probability. Therefore, by knowing the difficulty and discrimination of an item, we can begin to predict a student's level of ability from the answer (correct or incorrect). With a larger sample of items, the prediction gets more and more accurate. These data can also be used to construct tests with exactly the same item characteristics, although the items themselves are different.

Why Are These Concepts So Important?

Now that you have endured this section, you may be asking again, "This still seems awfully technical. Why do I have to know this?" We will apply the concepts elucidated here in later chapters, but let's discuss the basics now. By understanding these measurement concepts, you are becoming very aware that measurements have error. That means you must first consider these concepts and how they might affect each measure used with your students. Unfortunately, many teachers and parents believe, for instance, that standardized test scores always tell the *real* story. This is the one set of scores in which everyone tends to put all of their faith. Everyone believes that these standardized tests provide the true and complete analysis of the child's brain.

It is true that standardized tests are constructed with a great deal of care, and they tend to be of good to high quality. Also, they come with very official-looking reports. But now you should be realizing that no test is perfect for every situation or every child, and there is no such thing as a complete analysis of the child's brain. Accordingly, the key is how you use the scores. Remember every child's scores will not be of the same quality. Some scores will be more accurate than others. You must use all of the information you have gathered about a student to help you decide on the validity of any one piece of assessment data. Only once you have decided the scores are reliable and valid for the student can the information be used to improve your instruction.

Digging Deeper...

Some test publishers provide scoring options to give teachers some assistance in evaluating the reliability and validity of individual student scores. They have what is called an *invalid subtest*. A student's score can be considered invalid if any of the following criteria are met. (These may vary with publisher or test.)

- ◆ The student does not answer the first few items in the test section.
- ◆ The student does not answer any of the first few items correctly.
- ◆ The teacher marks the section invalid.

The rationales for these criteria are that students who do not answer the first items in a section (the easiest) most likely did not participate in that section (i.e., the entire section is blank and should not be scored). Students who do not get any of these easy items correct are either marking the answer sheet randomly, or the test may be an inappropriate level for them. Finally, if the teacher notices that the student is not participating in testing or is not able to finish because of illness, and so on, the section can be marked invalid. Use of this option in scoring will cause sections of the test not to be scored, thus avoiding the generation of scores that are of questionable reliability or validity.

The person administering the test and the people interpreting the results must evaluate the potential threats to the reliability and validity of each student's score. If you, as the main user of these scores, do not know the influences that can affect the scores, you cannot evaluate the potential threats to the accuracy of the scores. Now that you know that the fewer the number of items on a test, the less reliable it is (the less likely the student would get the same score if he or she took it repeatedly), you know to interpret short tests with caution, or at least to consider that limitation. Now that you know that tests must be valid, you can always ask yourself the questions: Does this score tell me what I think it does? Is this an accurate measure of this student's science skills? Did I find out what I needed to know?

Putting It into Practice

Scenario Nine—Andrew

You have decided to use performance on homework assignments to help you evaluate your students' ability to do proofs in geometry. Andrew turns in a week's worth of perfect homework assignments, and you are fairly confident his skills are where they should be. However, when you give the assessment for the end of the unit, Andrew's performance is much below what you would have expected.

What theories do you have to explain this discrepancy in performance? How might you go about checking them out?

Discussion

The first thing to think about is *which* assessment result is not valid? One way to get additional data is to ask Andrew to do a proof for you, and to explain his thinking as he goes along. If he has difficulty, you might tell him how surprised you are that he is struggling because he does so well on his homework assignments. You may find out that Andrew has been getting assistance from a parent or sibling at home, and this helper has been successful at providing a good proof, but unsuccessful at teaching Andrew to do it! This would mean the homework data were invalid.

Or, you may find that Andrew suffers from a form of test anxiety, which disables him during a stressful test situation, whereas he can perform the skill well in the privacy and quiet of his room at home. This would suggest Andrew's test result is invalid. In either case, you have additional information about Andrew and can make an appropriate decision about his instruction depending on what your findings were.

Summary

Now you are in the position of having the knowledge to consider the potential threats to the accuracy of your students' assessment scores, whether they are classroom assessments or state-mandated standardized tests. Because the issue of validity is so important, and because a score can only be valid if it is reliable, we will refer to these threats hereafter as *threats to validity*. Once you have ascertained that a student's score is probably valid (i.e., you can think of no obvious reason why it shouldn't be), you need to consider the score in relation to other information you have about the student. This is called using multiple measurements.

For example, consider a very low standardized test math computation score for a student who routinely demonstrates proficiency in math calculation in the classroom. If you used information from either of these assessment situations in isolation, you would come to very different conclusions about the student's skills. Acknowledging the discrepancies (or lack of them) between the results of several assessments is the first step in determining what must be done instructionally to improve the student's performance. A student whose performance is very consistent, regardless of the assessment situation or format, has more than likely provided you with valid assessment results. Students whose results vary obviously have some invalid results, and it is your mission to discover which are valid and which are not. Once you do, you can successfully address weaknesses the student may have that may be barriers to consistent, high performance.

We will be looking more at applications in validity in Chapters 5 and 6. Until then, congratulations on making it through measurement concepts! Your students will benefit from your persistence.

References

Cunningham, G. K. (1986). *Educational and psychological measurement.* New York: Macmillan.

Guilford, J. P., & Fruchter, B. (1978). *Fundamental statistics in psychology and education* (6th ed.). New York: McGraw-Hill.

Katz, L. (1997). *A developmental approach to assessment of young children.* East Lansing, MI: National Center for Research on Teacher Learning. (ERIC Digest No. 407172)

Lane, S., Wang, N., & Magone, M. (1996). Gender-related differential item functioning on a middle school mathematics performance assessment. *Educational Measurement: Issues and Practice, 15*(4), 21–27.

Langenfeld, T. E. (1997). Test fairness: Internal and external investigations of gender bias in mathematics testing. *Educational Measurement: Issues and Practice, 16*(1), 20–26.

Messick, S. (1989). Validity. In R. L. Linn (Ed.), *Educational measurement* (3rd ed., pp. 13–103). Washington, DC: American Council on Education & National Council on Measurement in Education.

Popham, W. J. (1997). Consequential validity: Right concern-wrong concept. *Educational Measurement: Issues and Practice, 16*(2), 9–13.

Shepard, L. A. (1997). The centrality of test use and consequences for test validity. *Educational Measurement: Issues and Practice, 16*(2), 5–8.

Thompson, B., & Vacha-Haase, T. (2000). Psychometrics is datametrics: The test is not reliable. *Educational and Psychological Measurement, 60*(2), 174–195.

Wainer, H. (1996). How is reliability related to the quality of test scores? What is the effect of local dependence on reliability? *Educational Measurement: Issues and Practice, 15*(1), 22–29.

Yen, W. (1993). Scaling performance assessments: Strategies for managing local item dependence. *Journal of Educational Measurement, 30,* 187–213.

4

Preparing
Your Students to Show
What They Know

Many professionals, from real estate agents to physicians, electricians to lawyers, must pass a standardized test to become certified to practice their profession. Students take the SAT or ACT to gain college admission. So, whether we like it or not, assessment, evaluation, and testing will be a significant part of students' life experiences. If we try to convince ourselves that we should protect students from "those nasty tests," we may actually be doing them a disservice by neglecting to adequately prepare them for the evaluations that await them in the future. Instead, we need to help students develop the skills they need to be able to show what they know on any assessment they take, regardless of the testing situation or format.

Putting It into Practice

Scenario Ten—Joyce

Joyce is a student who likes to write and is very good at it. Her language skills are good, her spelling is good, and she knows her capitalization and punctuation. You expect Joyce to perform very well on the language arts section of the norm-referenced test given in your school. But Joyce's scores are only average. Before coming to a final conclusion about the validity of the norm-referenced test scores, you decide to find out a little more about the test. The language arts test includes a section on editing. Students must read a selection of sentences and identify the one written correctly or incorrectly. Another type of item has the same sentence written several different ways, and students must pick the one that is written correctly. Most of these items focus on finding errors in capitalization, punctuation, and grammar. Joyce's scores indicate that editing was her area of weakness. From what you know, do you think Joyce's score in language is valid? Are there any threats to validity you can think of?

Discussion

Chances are that Joyce's score is valid. This assessment is asking her to do something that she rarely does: Edit work containing errors. Joyce gets no practice editing because she generates correct work to begin with. When she reads her own work, there are no errors for her to find. In the test, when errors are present, she has difficulty seeing them; in some cases, these students self-correct as they read without realizing it. Then they cannot identify where the errors are. Unfortunately for these students, often one of the options in editing test items is that the sentence is correct as it is written. Students without an eye for errors will often choose that option. It may be helpful to look at some actual items with Joyce to test this theory. Joyce may need some practice editing so she can develop the eye to spot errors. It may help her to edit the work of a partner so she gets some practice. She may also benefit from experiences with multiple-choice editing items.

Test-Taking Skills

An important goal of assessment is to obtain accurate information about what students know and can do. Therefore, we want to reduce the effects of any other factors that may get in the way of performance (threats to validity). We have discussed many factors that may influence a student's ability to perform well in a testing situation. We want all students to be well prepared to show what they know on the test, and to reduce the potential measurement error caused by these other factors.

Students with poor test-taking skills may not do well because of their unfamiliarity with the test, and not because they do not know the content. Therefore, the teaching of test-taking skills will allow you to reduce the effects of unfamiliarity. The purpose of having these skills is to reduce irrelevant variance in scores (Mehrens, Popham, & Ryan, 1998). So how can you teach your students test-taking skills without losing time you need to teach the curriculum?

We spoke earlier of teaching to the test. Hopefully, you are able to consider this issue in a different light now. When preparing students for a valued assessment, one that assesses the curriculum they are to be learning, teaching to the test is what is expected. This is because a valued assessment measures a curriculum where parents, community, and business people would say, "Yes! I want students to know and be able to do these things." But always keep in mind the distinction between teaching to the test and cheating. Cheating is providing students with information to help them perform well on the test even though they do not have the skills being assessed. If you begin to lose perspective of what constitutes cheating, refer back to the examples provided in Chapter 1.

In this section, we will assume that the state or local assessments required have a certain amount of relationship to the curriculum being taught, and the content of the assessment is valued. Therefore, we will not focus directly on the content of the assessments but on some of the other important issues. These involve preparing the students to do the best job they can to demonstrate what they know on the assessment. Some people would refer to these as *test-taking skills*.

Teaching test-taking skills can have the same negative connotation as teaching to the test when discussed by the public, rightly so when it is done at the expense of teaching the curriculum. How many times have we heard of classroom activities being suspended two weeks prior to testing so that students can be prepared for the upcoming test? Not only is this disruptive, but it provides a poor example to students and the community by reducing valuable instructional time. Most test-taking strategies can be taught by incorporating them into regular classroom activities all during the school year. In many ways, by developing these skills, you will be helping to develop problem-solving skills and thinking skills in your students that will benefit them every day, as well as when they take various admissions tests and professional licensing exams.

Test-taking skills should provide students with the test information they need to be able to show what they know. If the teaching of test-taking skills threatens the validity of the assessment (i.e., students are taught tricks to help them answer correctly when they do not know the information being assessed), then test preparation has gone too far.

It can be very motivating for students when their teacher teams up with them to help them beat the test. Gone are the days when students should be seeing the process of assessment as "me against the teacher," a "total mystery," or "guess what the teacher is thinking." Nowadays, students should approach assessment as a chance for "my teacher and me to team up to prepare me to show what I know."

Tips for Preparing Students to Show What They Know

Call it problem solving, thinking skills, test-taking skills, or test preparation, but do it every day as part of your regular instruction. Start by making sure your students are learning the curriculum. (We will go into more detail about that later.) Expose them to all types of item formats, and be creative to get your students thinking. Here are some different questions to ask your students relative to the strategies they use to answer multiple-choice questions (see Questions to Ask about a Multiple-Choice Question). These questions will help you to get more useful information about how your students are thinking about what you are teaching, as well as develop their multiple-choice test-taking strategies.

First, develop or choose a good quality multiple-choice item that assesses some content the students have learned recently. Second, instead of asking students to select the best answer, choose an alternative method of student response. You may choose a response strategy from those listed here or use one you have developed yourself.

Questions to Ask about a Multiple-Choice Question

- Sam chose A. Decide whether or not you think he is correct. Justify your answer.

- Choose the best answer. Explain the strategy you used to eliminate two of the incorrect choices.

- Marie chose B. Write a paragraph to explain what mistakes you think Marie may have made.

- Choose the best answer. Write a note to your friend to explain how you made your decision. Include a reason why you chose the answer.

- How are the answer choices alike? Give two ways the answer choices are alike. Give two ways the answer choices are different. Which answer is correct?

- Carole answered this question incorrectly. Which incorrect answer do you think fooled her? Explain why you chose your answer.

- Read the question. Eliminate as many of the incorrect answers as you can. Explain the process you used to eliminate the incorrect answers.

- Explain what this question is asking. What do you think the correct answer is? Do any of the other answers seem reasonable? Explain why or why not.

Use these questions as quick warm-ups, and allow students time to discuss their strategies in small groups and then as a class. This will give students who have difficulty a chance to learn the strategies others use to approach multiple-choice questions. During their discussion, you will also get valuable information about the students' level of knowledge and skill with the content area being assessed. You will most likely get some insight into what misconceptions they have or errors they are making and be able to correct them on the spot. How much more efficient could one item be?

Conduct similar activities with performance assessments. Every now and then, use one as a class or small group activity. Discuss with the students the different ways to approach the problem presented. Always conduct these activities with assessment tools whose content is relevant to what the students have been learning. That way, the activity doubles as a tool for you to assess your students' learning.

Summary List of Tips for Teachers

Here is a short list summarizing some tips for teaching your students to be good test takers.

- ♦ Always demonstrate a positive attitude toward the assessment, regardless of how you may actually feel.
- ♦ Create a partnership with students to demystify tests for them.
- ♦ In class, explain as often as possible why incorrect answers are incorrect.
- ♦ Give students practice with timed activities—teach them how to pace themselves.
- ♦ Model problem-solving strategies with students.
- ♦ Talk through how to determine what a question is asking.
- ♦ Encourage explanations of how students choose answers or approach problems.
- ♦ Teach students different ways questions can be asked (backwards thinking, inclusion of irrelevant information, etc.).
- ♦ Talk about strategies used to eliminate incorrect answer choices.
- ♦ When teaching concepts such as number sense, estimation, and other skills useful in test taking, remind students to use them on tests.
- ♦ Make sure students are familiar with a variety of item formats.
- ♦ Discuss how to choose "one best answer" with students.

Now that you have some ideas about how to develop test-taking skills with your students, we will discuss teacher-made tests. There are many very good books and articles written about test construction, item development, writing performance assessments, and so on. This section will not attempt to duplicate those resources here. Instead, it will discuss a little bit about the considerations that must be given to the measurement integrity of classroom assessments.

The Classroom Assessment

All of the state and locally mandated assessments available cannot assure that a student will learn the content required by a school's curriculum. This is because the most meaningful, relevant assessment is done every day by the classroom teacher. Much of the care and measurement expertise is reserved for standardized tests, when, in fact, we should be making sure that the most important assessments, the ones used in the classroom, are of as high a quality as possible.

Standards of Assessment Quality

Richard Stiggins (2000) has published a list of standards for assessments. These requirements may seem daunting, yet think of the strict requirements we have for standardized test publishers. Their products are used much less frequently and often with less impact than the assessments designed, administered, and scored by teachers every day.

Addressing this list of five standards of assessment quality should be the goal of every classroom teacher. You should make use of these standards to evaluate the quality of your classroom assessments. Stiggins lists the standards as follows:

1. Quality assessments arise from and accurately reflect clearly specified and appropriate achievement expectations for students.

2. Sound assessments are specifically designed to serve instructional purposes.

3. Quality assessments accurately reflect the intended target and serve the intended purpose.

4. Quality assessments provide a representative sample of student performance that is sufficient in its scope to permit confident conclusions about student achievement.

5. Sound assessments are designed, developed, and used in such a manner as to eliminate sources of bias or distortion that interfere with the accuracy of results.

The important point about these standards is that not meeting them means that the validity of the assessment is in jeopardy. The result may not be the information that was intended. So what can a teacher do to make sure that classroom assessments meet the standards outlined by Stiggins?

First, spend a little more time in designing your assessments and pay attention to how successful (or unsuccessful) they are with your students. Here are some areas to which you should pay particular attention.

Developing Your Own Assessments

This section is not meant to be a complete primer on assessment development. There are many very well-written, comprehensive resources to assist you with making up your own tests. Check the bibliography for some samples. However, there are some considerations you must be aware of when you develop your own assessments because these considerations can enhance or threaten the validity of your students' results.

Selecting Formats

Anytime something new is introduced in education, there seems to be a rush to drop the old and pick up the new. With the introduction of performance-based instruction and assessment, some teachers dropped the selected response items (multiple choice, matching, true-false) in favor of performance assessment for every test or assignment.

Probably a better approach would be to add performance assessment to the resources we already have in our assessment toolboxes. After all, multiple-choice tests are still alive and well, and those item types must have some good use or purpose! The fact of the matter is that we just don't always need a student to complete a time-consuming performance task to see if they have learned. Multiple-choice items can be written to assess skills of a higher order than mere recall. Because multiple choice and other selected response items require less response time, they allow a larger sample of items to be included. We have learned from our study of measurement concepts that this will result in a more reliable, valid assessment of students. Multiple-choice items are also efficient and easy to score.

It is therefore important that the teacher carefully select an appropriate item type for each concept to be assessed. If you need to know if your students know their multiplication facts, there is no need to give them a 45-minute performance assessment. Instead, give them a sample of short answer multiplication fact problems, or ask them to generate a multiplication table. Be sure to vary the types of questions you use so that students are familiar with every item type. Most important, the item type selected should be consistent with the target of the instruction. If students were being taught to write, they should not be assessed by selecting responses—they must write.

Sampling Appropriately

Have you ever taken a test and come away saying "That is not what I expected at all! The whole test was about obscure little details. It didn't represent what we concentrated on in class!" This is a result of a sampling problem, and you were questioning content or face validity. What you were led to believe was the important points were not assessed. This also can happen when an entire assessment consists of one or two essays. If the topics covered on the assessment were the only ones your students didn't emphasize in their study, you are going to come to the conclusion that they know very little, although that is not necessarily the case.

The problem with sampling is that when you give your students a selection of items and call it an assessment, you expect to generalize how they perform on those few items to make a judgment of what they learned about the topics covered. If those few items are not representative of what was emphasized in class, or what is valued for the student to know, that generalization may not be valid. Therefore, deciding what is important to include in the assessment is a very important step to guaranteeing the validity of your assessment results. It will sometimes help to go back to the objectives and targets you had for your lessons. Avoid testing obscure facts and picayune details. Try to include as large a sample of items as possible. Short answer and selected response can help you by adding opportunities for students to show what they know without adding a lot of time to the total assessment. Of course, you should not add items for the sake of lengthening the test, if the domain of what you wanted your students to learn can be quickly and easily assessed in a few items; by all means, limit your test to those few items.

Remember that a very important advantage to a teacher-developed test is that it can be tailored to the concepts taught. There is no excuse for a teacher to include material on a test that was not covered in instruction. All of your students need to have been given the opportunity to learn the assessed material, either in assigned readings or in classroom activities.

Avoiding Bias

With some knowledge about your students and some careful thought, avoiding test bias in a classroom assessment is much easier than it is for a national test publisher. The national test publisher must consider all possible types of bias. As long as you are willing to be open to potential bias in any of your items, you really need only to be concerned with the students in your class. And just as you must make appropriate instructional decisions because you know these children, you can review your test items for bias for each special case in your class. If you have a child in your class who does not celebrate birthdays for religious reasons, assessing students' knowledge of statistics using a survey of the class's birthday celebration preferences may be biased against that child. But if everyone does celebrate birthdays, the potential for bias is less.

The important responsibility is that you review the test through each child's eyes. Does this item favor girls? Will the educationally disadvantaged students in the class know what DVD movies are? Will this topic make the Asian students uncomfortable? After the test is administered, another look, this time with the benefit of student responses, can sometimes reveal problems that were not apparent previously. If you do find items that you think favor one student over others, the item should be removed from the test, *and* the scores should be adjusted appropriately.

Administration Issues

More and more classrooms have some students with special needs. These students may have disabilities, or they may not yet speak English fluently. In either case, they may require the use of some accommodations to assess them accurately. Accommodations are meant to level the playing field for these students because they help compensate for the disability or limitation with English. Accommodations should not provide students with an advantage over other students.

In standardized testing situations, accommodations may result in invalid test scores, because of the type of test. (Norm-referenced tests require that all students take the test under the same conditions as the norm group so that performance can be compared to the norm group.) But in classroom instruction and assessments, modifications can help to assure the accuracy or validity of assessment results. Let's discuss some specific examples.

You want to assess your students' knowledge and ability in the area of mathematics word problems. You want them to read the problem, solve it, and write a paragraph explaining the approach they used to solve the problem.

Doris has a disability, and she cannot read yet. Marco is just learning English, and although he understands it, he cannot read or write it. Both students are learning mathematics at their given grade level. Remember that we want to know what Doris and Marco know about word problems in mathematics. How should the assessment be administered to them? What will happen if Doris and Marco sit with the rest of their class and take this assessment? Chances are they will do very poorly. Is this because they do not know the mathematics being assessed? Or is it because they cannot read the problems? We will not know. However, if the test is read aloud to these two students, we will know that their lack of reading skill did not interfere with their ability to perform the mathematics. Then we can be more comfortable knowing that if they do not do well, it is the mathematics they do not know, and our instruction can be planned accordingly. The accommodation was reasonable in this case because we were not testing reading (although reading does compose a part of the total task), we wanted to know what the students know about mathematics.

Later in the week, the same students take a reading assessment. Should the reading assessment be read to Doris and Marco? Again, that depends on the purpose of the assessment. If the assessment is designed to measure reading ability, then to read the assessment to the two students would provide them with an unfair advantage. After all, the test is testing whether or not they can read! Therefore, because Doris and Marco cannot read, low test results would be accurate in this case. However, what if the test were assessing how well students could explain how a character in a story was feeling or what would happen next in the story? This is more of an applied reading skill. To assess whether Doris and Marco can answer these types of questions, it may be acceptable to allow the story and questions to be read to them. Keep in mind, however, that regardless of how Doris and Marco perform on the mathematics test and the applied reading test, they still can't read and their instructional program must include a heavy dose of reading until they can.

Putting It into Practice

Scenario Eleven—Kim

Kim is a student who has just arrived in this country. He knows very little English and has been enrolled in a program for students for whom English is a second language. Lately, Kim has been acting out in class, and the school psychologist has been called in to assess Kim for an emotional disability. The psychologist administers several assessments and comes to the conclusion that Kim is emotionally disabled. Do you think this assessment is likely to be valid? What are potential threats to the validity of Kim's results?

Discussion

There is a distinct possibility that Kim could not adequately understand the assessment items he took. He speaks limited English and is likely to have misinterpreted the assessment. Furthermore, from a cultural standpoint, the assessments may have included concepts that are second-nature to a student raised in the United States but may be totally foreign to this student. Most likely, it would be a disservice to Kim to label him emotionally disabled on the basis of the assessments alone. It is doubtful that his assessment results are valid.

Scenario Twelve—Susan

Susan is a sixth grader who has great difficulty reading. Her school requires each student's reading comprehension to be assessed using a standard, multiple-choice reading test. While Susan's class is taking the test, an instructional aide notices that Susan is very frustrated. She moves Susan to another area and reads the test aloud to her.

Is Susan's score a valid indication of her reading comprehension ability? Why or why not?

Discussion

The purpose of this test was to assess reading comprehension. The instructional aide, while trying to be kind, provided an accommodation that served to invalidate the test. A test result must be considered invalid any time the testing circumstances do not allow a proper administration. In this case, the student was provided with inappropriate assistance during a testing situation. In many schools, this would be considered cheating. It also would be of no benefit to Susan, because her score will be higher than it should be, and she may not get the instructional help she needs.

Some accommodations will not be allowed for certain tests because the accommodation invalidates the test. For example, if a state requires students to demonstrate reading proficiency to graduate, any accommodation that helps the student to read when they do not have those skills should not be allowed. Therefore, even though a special education student may have an accommodation that allows them to have all assessments read to them, they may not be allowed to have a test read to them because the purpose of the test is to assess reading ability. Reading the test to the student allows them the possibility to pass the test although they can't read. This would result in a test score that is inaccurate.

The situation is more complicated for Susan, however, because she is not enrolled in a special education program and has no allowable accommodations. What should the aide have done? Susan could have been encouraged to continue the test after being assured that she was not expected to know every answer. It would have been even more desirable to give Susan a test that was more on her reading level, especially if the test is meant to provide diagnostic information for instruction. However, this is not always possible when a test is required by the school or school system. Sometimes, assessments may just not seem to be fair to all students, but if Susan's poor performance gets her the instructional help she needs, the final outcome may be a good one.

The important point is to be aware of the purpose of each assessment and plan accommodations based on that purpose. Do not compromise an assessment by giving a student an advantage with any skill that they must demonstrate on the assessment. We want all of our students to do well, but their performance should reflect actual skill, not our pity. Keep in mind that some of the freedom you have to do the right thing in classroom assessment may be taken away from you for mandated or No Child Left Behind (NCLB) assessments, especially for students without disabilities.

What about the student who cannot write? Some students have disabilities that keep them from being able to translate their thoughts onto paper. Sometimes, these students dictate their responses to someone else who records them. If this is the only way the student can transfer thoughts, it does not provide him or her with an unfair advantage. The availability of reasonable accommodations must not take the place of appropriate instruction in the areas of weakness. They merely allow valid assessment of other areas until the weakness has been addressed.

Other accommodations are less likely to influence a test score's validity. These are accommodations such as preferential seating in the room (e.g., for a hearing-impaired student), breaks during the test, administration of an assessment by a specific examiner, such as the English as a Second Language teacher or the Special Education teacher, or assistance recording responses on an answer sheet (i.e., student points to answer, and recorder marks that answer on the answer sheet). All of these types of accommodations allow special needs students to participate in assessments and obtain valid scores. Accommodations should never be used just for assessments; the same accommodations should be used during regular instruction so that students are familiar with the procedures they will use on an assessment. Also, if the student does not need the accommodation every day, he or she does not need it for a test.

The advantage of using accommodations in the classroom is that the teacher decides how to best get the most accurate information possible for each student. The challenge is to remember that these accommodations may not always be available to students, especially to those without documented disabilities, so they must be used only as required and should be discontinued as soon as possible. Allowing unnecessary accommodations will cause a student to become dependent and may provide inflated assessment results that will be discrepant with outside assessments.

Scoring Basics

The purpose of this book is not to address the detailed issues of scoring assessments. There are many references and resources on this extensive and complex topic. (See the Bibliography for examples.) However, there are a few points that need to be made about scoring classroom assessments because they directly relate to the accuracy of the information generated. We will discuss the scoring of constructed response items first.

When a teacher makes up a test, the correct answers should be developed at the same time. In other words, it is important to know what response is expected of the students. This activity often helps in good test development, because test items can be refined to make sure they elicit the expected response from students (i.e., if you want three reasons, ask for three reasons). Compare each response to a standard; avoid letting the responses you get define the top and bottom score. This way, if all of the students hit the mark, all should receive full credit. If some students do better than the standard, great; but students should not be penalized or receive lower scores because of other students' outstanding performance.

Try to use some form of analytic scoring. Analytic scoring is scoring done in parts or units. For example, an essay may be scored for several different criteria: content, accuracy, and organization; and grammar, punctuation, and spelling. This type of scoring provides more detailed information to the student because it allows him or her to see where improvement is needed. It also allows the teacher to see where instruction is needed. If Kim's essay is accurate and well organized, but contains spelling and grammar errors, she needs different instruction than Karen, whose essay contains many content errors. In addition, Cizek (2000) reports that students learn more when they have information about their strengths and weaknesses, and "analytic scoring is more appropriate for those purposes."

The other type of scoring, not as informative as analytic, but sometimes used in the interest of time or to evaluate the quality of the whole product, is holistic scoring. In holistic scoring, one grade is assigned that takes all aspects of the scoring into account.

Another important aspect of scoring involves efficiency. Suppose, for example, your students write an essay explaining three reasons why the colonies won the Revolutionary War. You plan to score the essay for content related to history and social studies skills. But what would keep you from using that same essay to score students on their writing progress and perhaps, even on language usage (capitalization, punctuation, grammar, etc.) In that one essay, you have tripled the amount of assessment information gained by scoring the essay three different ways with three different standards or sets of criteria. Consider how much the student may be showing you of what he or she knows because what is demonstrated may not be limited to the original intent of the question. Of course, if you plan to grade an essay for several different skills, students should be informed ahead of time.

An Introduction to Using Assessment Data

Once you have administered and scored your assessment, you are ready to begin your evaluation of the results. It is important to take a critical look at the assessment before you look at student results to plan your future instruction. Sometimes this will be an informal look at the assessment, sometimes it will be more formal. The following sections will give you guidelines to tell you what to look for.

Item Analysis

Scoring of selected response items is straightforward and objective. Students answer the item either correctly or incorrectly. How can the teacher use this information in any way other than a total test score? Let's think back to Chapter 3 where we discussed item difficulty and item discrimination. Not only can these concepts help us evaluate the quality of a test, they can also help us to learn more about the errors our students make.

Remember that item difficulty is an indication of how difficult the item was for the group tested. Item difficulty is simply the number of students who answer correctly divided by the number of students answering the item. If every student answers correctly, item difficulty will be a one. If no students answer correctly, item difficulty will be zero.

Item discrimination is an indication of how effective the item is at distinguishing between students who know the material tested and those who do not. We are going to take an informal approach and demonstrate how you can use these concepts to evaluate one of your multiple-choice tests.

What is a good item difficulty value? That depends on the purpose of the test. If the test was designed to assess whether students have mastered a set of skills, and the expectation is that all students will answer all or mostly all of the items correctly, high difficulty levels (indicating easy items, or items all students answered correctly) would be expected. However, if the purpose of the assessment is to separate those who know the material from those who do not, lower item difficulty levels (more difficult items) would be acceptable. Item difficulty is dependent on the group taking the test, so difficulty values from one class of students, such as a high-achieving group, may be quite different from those from a struggling group.

Figure 4.1 summarizes results from a class of ten students on a test of ten items.

Figure 4.1. Sample Item Analysis Data: Difficulty Level

		Number of Students Choosing Each Answer					
Item Number	Answer Key	A	B	C	D	Number of Students	Item Difficulty
1	B	0	**10**	0	0	10	1.00
2	A	**8**	1	1	0	10	0.80
3	C	6	1	**3**	0	10	0.30
4	B	2	**8**	0	0	10	0.80
5	D	3	2	0	**5**	10	0.50
6	A	**9**	0	0	1	10	0.90
7	C	2	1	**6**	1	10	0.60
8	B	0	**5**	5	0	10	0.50
9	D	1	4	3	**2**	10	0.20
10	A	**5**	1	1	3	10	0.50
Number of students with correct answer is indicated in boldface.							

The teacher who made this table merely counted up the number of students choosing each possible response for each item. Incorrect responses are referred to as *distractors*. The job of a distractor is to pull the attention of a student unsure of the answer away from the correct answer by providing a plausible, yet less than best answer for the item. In many cases, the distractor is less than plausible, but it represents a common error made by students who have not yet mastered the skill.

The item difficulty is in the far right column of the table. When we look at the item difficulty, we notice right away that four items have a difficulty of .80 or higher. This means that at least 80 percent of the students got these items correct. (Item 6 actually had 90 percent of students answering correctly, and item 1 had all students answer correctly.) These items are considered easy because almost everyone answered them correctly. We also notice that there are two items (3 and 9) that appear difficult, that is, not many students answered them correctly. In fact, only two of the ten students answered item 9 correctly. Items 5, 7, 8, and 10 had difficulty indicators in the moderate range.

What can this information tell us? It depends. In looking at the numbers of students who chose each distractor, some different patterns emerge. We already noticed that all students answered item 1 correctly. This could be because all students know that information. It could also be that the other answer choices were ineffective in providing a distraction to students unsure of the answer. Some teachers even build in a give-away distractor, usually a nonsense answer that every student can eliminate from consideration. A better practice would be to reduce the number of plausible distractors and avoid nonsense distractors.

Let's assume that item 1's distractors were all plausible, but all of the students really knew this material. This item appears to have functioned as expected. How about item 3? The correct answer was C, but only three students chose that response. Instead, six students chose A, and one chose B. It appears that the class did not know the answer to this item. They may have an error in their thinking, causing them to choose distractor A. If so, the error represented by distractor A will require special emphasis in instruction.

Item 9 is also a difficult item, but has a different pattern of errors than item 3. Instead of a majority of students choosing one distractor, student choices are scattered a bit more among the distractors in item 9. It would appear that students were unsure of the correct answer, and all of the distractors seemed plausible. This pattern suggests the possibility that the students were not taught the concept being assessed. At least it strongly suggests that the students didn't learn the concept even if it was taught. This is certainly a case for reteaching. But what if the students just didn't understand the question? That would be quickly discovered during instruction, and the proper action would be to rewrite or eliminate the confusing item from the total test score.

Continue your study of the results. Look at items 5, 8, and 10. All three have difficulty levels of 0.50, but how do they differ?

By now, you might be wondering if it would be helpful if you knew *who* was answering each of these items correctly. You are beginning to think critically about assessment results and have anticipated our next analysis!

Your question refers to the issue of discrimination. What you want to know is whether or not the students who did well overall on the test answered some of these items incorrectly. What you are probably thinking is that if the low-achieving students are answering incorrectly, the results of the analysis are less bothersome than if the high-achieving students are answering incorrectly. Let's examine the data in Figure 4.2.

Figure 4.2. Sample Item Analysis Data: Discrimination

Item Performance											
Students	Total Score	#1	#2	#3	#4	#5	#6	#7	#8	#9	#10
Ann	10	*	*	*	*	*	*	*	*	*	*
Clarissa	9	*	*	*	*	*	*	*	*	B	*
Maureen	9	*	*	A	*	*	*	*	*	*	*
Liz	8	*	*	A	*	*	*	*	*	B	*
Baxter	7	*	*	A	*	*	D	*	*	B	*
Jill	5	*	*	*	A	A	*	*	C	B	B
Mike	4	*	*	A	*	B	*	A	C	C	C
Bob	3	*	*	A	A	A	*	A	C	A	D
Irene	3	*	B	A	*	B	*	B	C	C	D
Jack	2	*	C	B	*	A	*	D	C	C	D
* indicates correct response											
A, B, C, or D = incorrect response (corresponding to response chosen)											

Students are listed in order of their test scores, highest to lowest. Only one student, Ann, answered all of the items correctly. Along the top of the table, the item numbers are listed, 1 to 10. The body of the table indicates whether the student answered correctly (*), and if not, which distractor was chosen (A, B, C, or D).

If you draw an imaginary line across the middle of the table (just below Baxter), you divide the class into the top half of scorers and the bottom half of scorers. Now let's look and see where the mistakes are. First you may notice that items 3 and 9 were problems for some of the high scorers. And they were all distracted by the same response (option A for item 3 and option B for item 9). This is potentially useful information because students with demonstrated knowledge were all drawn to the same incorrect option. Is there an element of truth to either of these options? What happens if these students are asked to explain why they chose these options? Do they demonstrate they all have a common misconception, or was there a misunderstanding of what the item was asking? This is very important information for both test item evaluation as well as instructional planning for these students. (Do they really need additional instruction?)

Think back to your initial analysis of items 5, 8, and 10. Does this new information help you? Notice that the five students scoring the highest on the test answered these three items correctly, whereas the low scorers answered them incorrectly. This would suggest that these items are effective at discriminating between those who know the material and those who do not. How does item 8 stand out? It looks as if the students who answered this item incorrectly all have the same misconception. At least they were all drawn by the same distractor. This may indicate a straightforward instructional intervention for those five students.

Putting It into Practice

Scenario Thirteen—Sixth Grade Social Studies

You are reading through a performance assessment that you just administered to your sixth grade social studies class. They were to predict some characteristics of a newly discovered culture from some information about the environment they live in (topography, climate, access to water, etc.). The first paper you read is just fine until you get to question five. The response the student supplied is not at all what you had expected when you wrote the question and drafted your *exemplary response* (the response you were looking for). It is obvious that the student did not understand what you expected to be entered into a chart provided. You assign zero points to the chart, finish grading the paper, and move on. In the group of 25 papers, a similar problem is evident with a total of 22 papers.

Did you get a valid measure of what you intended to assess in question five? What should you do with the test results?

Discussion

Congratulations! What you have done is an informal item analysis. And you have discovered an item that was ineffective at assessing the information you wanted to assess. Therefore, you do not have the information you wanted, and the item does not provide you with valid information for the majority of the class. You must do two things: first, come up with another way to find out if the students learned the skill you intended to assess; and second, adjust the results so that they are not artificially lowered by the ineffective item.

Remember that the first student received zero points for the response given. Chances are, so did the other 22 students who misunderstood the item. You may think that because almost everyone got it wrong, the playing field is even, and the item can be left in the test. But this provides confusing feedback to students. You and your students will learn a lot in a discussion of what you were thinking when the item was written and what they were thinking when they responded to it. The discussion you have with your students may also include asking for their suggestions for how to rewrite the item so that students are more likely to give the response you are expecting. That way, you'll have the feedback you need to modify the item for use with another group of students in the future.

Next, you must go back and recalculate results. The students will feel that they have been treated fairly if the item is removed from the assessment, and they are not penalized (even if it would have been equally) for being misled by the item. This thought panics teachers who feel they need that perfect number of items or points to make the gradebook work out easily. But this need should not be favored over the students' need for valid results and fairness.

Hopefully, you have seen some of the advantages to this type of analysis. You may identify test items that aren't effective or are confusing to students. You may be able to tell more about the errors that your students are making than you thought possible with a multiple-choice test. You can evaluate the effectiveness of your distractors. You can use the same technique to study the performance of items with various groups. Instead of grouping students by total score, also group them by gender, ethnic group, and so on, to explore patterns of responses.

If you find an item (or more) that clearly did not work the way you intended, it should be eliminated from the test, and student scores should be adjusted accordingly. Again, this demonstrates a wonderful advantage to classroom assessment! If an item doesn't work, it can be taken out of the test. This should encourage teachers to take some risks with their assessments, knowing that a disaster does not have to negatively impact the students, and a success can open up some new possibilities. This can provide a wonderful opportunity for growth.

Obviously, these analyses are a lot of work, and you will not be able to do them for each and every test you give every year. But the activity helps to train a teacher as to what works and what doesn't work in assessment, and this type of close scrutiny of a test can be quite valuable staff development. Item analysis can be very useful when student test results are not what you expected, or when you are experimenting with new formats or a new group of students.

Providing Useful Feedback

The most noble purpose of assessment is to provide feedback to both the student *and* the teacher. There are ways of doing this that can enhance future performance and instruction. Most important, if students are to use assessment results to improve their performance, they must be able to understand what they would have to do to obtain a higher score on the next assessment. An effective way to do this is to make sure students know what scoring or grading criteria are being used and to use the criteria when providing feedback. Rather than covering a student's work with red ink, it will probably be more useful to the student (although not always popular with them) to ask them to go through their work or work with a partner to find errors. Feedback is constructive and instructional, whereas grading or evaluating is providing a judgment. It is easier to receive feedback than it is to receive a judgment or evaluation.

Consider your own case as a teacher. If you consider what you discover about your students' learning as feedback in a process to get them where they need to be, it is much more constructive than to have your principal use the information as a judgment of your success as a teacher. Judgment implies it is all over, feedback assumes the process continues.

Now, of course there does come the time for assigning grades. A good reference for your further study about assigning grades is Robert Marzano's book, *Transforming Classroom Grading.* The key to effective grading practice for students is the same as the goal for teachers and the results of assessments. There should be no surprises. If students are well informed about the standards being used, they should be aware of the progress they have made, and they should be able to predict their grades. But for teachers, the use of assessment data for assigning the grade may be very different from the information they will use to plan future instruction.

Let's take an age-old example. You ask your students to write up a lab report on the experiment they conducted in science. You plan to use the report as an assessment of their skills in scientific writing, and when the rubric is shared, you point out to them that *spelling counts!* As you read the papers, you notice that some students are misspelling words, even words that are spelled correctly in the directions to the assignment. Because spelling counts in the rubric, you notice that some students are getting lower scores on their science paper, not because of their skills in science, but because of their lack of attention to spelling. The instructional implications for these students are obvious.

The important issue to remember here is the observation you made while scoring these papers. Incorrect spelling requires different instructional interventions than problems with the concepts of science assessed. These students understood the science, but they need help with their spelling. Their science grade, therefore, may not be an accurate reflection of their knowledge of science. It is this extension of thinking that is needed to become an effective interpreter of assessment results.

Summary

Very early in this book, the issue of time was discussed. This chapter provided some tips to assist teachers to equip students with test-taking skills by weaving them into everyday instruction. This means that the curriculum can be covered right up to testing day, thereby maximizing instructional time. Well-constructed classroom assessments are essential to this preparation. Evaluating the validity of classroom assessments can seem like a daunting task. But with a little practice, it becomes second nature, and with a lot of practice, you will be able to foresee problems and fix them before the test is ever administered. To help you get started, here is a simple checklist of questions you should consider for every classroom assessment you design.

- Does the assessment include the content I need to assess?
- Do all items assess essential content?
- Does the assessment adequately sample the content?
- Are the item formats appropriate for what is to be assessed?
- Have I considered all students in my review for possible item bias?
- Did any items show potential bias?
- Do I have enough items to have reliable scores?
- Did the students have enough time to finish the assessment?
- Is there evidence that any of the questions were not understood by the students?
- Were there any questions none of the students answered correctly?
- Did any items seem too hard for students who seemed to know the material?
- Did the scoring work? Was the exemplary response on target?
- Are these the results I expected from the students?
- Did I provide feedback to the students about their performance?

The answers to these questions will help you to make sure that your students' assessment data are valid. The NCLB Act makes it clear that we must meet the instructional needs of every student. To do that, we must be able to make good, informed instructional decisions based on valid assessment data.

If the data are flawed, our instructional decision-making will be flawed, too, and we will leave children behind.

Our next step, which we will take in Chapter 5, is to gain additional practice with some actual assessment results.

References

Cizek, G. L. (2000). Pockets of resistance in the assessment revolution. *Educational Measurement: Issues and Practice, 19*(2), 16–23.

Mehrens, W., Popham, W. J., & Ryan, J. (1998). How to prepare students for performance assessments. *Educational Measurement, 17,* 18–22.

Stiggins, R. J. (2000). *Where is our assessment future and how can we get there from here?* Paper presented at the Assessment in Educational Reform: Both Means and Ends Conference, University of Maryland, College Park, MD, June 5–6, 2000.

5

Threats to Validity

Before we can use assessment information to determine instructional needs, we must assure ourselves that the information is accurate (reliable and valid). In this chapter, you will get a chance to apply what you have learned so far to make that determination. In other words, you are going to practice thinking critically, like a measurement expert, about some students' test results. Then you will be able to analyze the assessment results of your own students in a similar way.

First, let us review what we mean by "threats to validity." Remember that all measures have some sort of measurement error. If this measurement error is significant enough to produce a result that is not a true or accurate representation of a student's skill, then the results cannot be used to plan further instruction for that student. A threat to validity is any situation, occurrence, or characteristic of an assessment that might be expected to keep the results of the assessment from being a measure of the skill it was intended to measure.

Many teachers can accurately predict how a student will perform on an assessment. They know that the assessment may not allow the student to show what he or she knows, but will administer the assessment anyway and use the results. It is important for teachers to be aware of the accuracy of any assessment result and to consider that accuracy when making instructional decisions for students. Testing administered to meet the requirements of No Child Left Behind (NCLB) may sometimes fit this situation. Although the teacher knows that a student is not a proficient reader, the state's testing program will require the student to participate in a test that is too difficult for him, and to receive a score (in this case, most likely valid). In other cases, a student struggling to learn English will have to take a mathematics test written in English, which may not allow the student to demonstrate what she knows about mathematics. That score may be used to determine adequate yearly progress for the school, but it should not be used to plan mathematics instruction for the student.

Identifying Threats to Validity

Some of the scenarios we will use should be familiar because they are similar to situations used as examples in the earlier parts of the book. This section will serve as a review of some key concepts before we move on to instructional planning. For each of the following scenarios, you will be answering these two questions (or a close variation):

1. Did this assessment result in a valid assessment of the skills being measured?
2. What are potential threats to validity?

The discussion section following each scenario will provide some sample ideas and possible solutions. Please keep in mind that the discussion section is not meant to be all-inclusive, but it will focus on the most obvious conclusions. Hopefully, you will have additional ideas. It will always be necessary to thoroughly test your conclusions to make sure you have made an accurate analysis.

Scenario One—Bill

Bill is a good student in your algebra class. He does his assignments and gets high scores on the tests. You are surprised when you record the scores from the most recent quiz you administered to the class because Bill received an uncharacteristically low score. When you enter the grade into your gradebook, you notice that Bill had been absent from class the three sessions just prior to the quiz. Most of the problems on the quiz focused on skills taught in those three class sessions.

Is Bill's quiz score an accurate reflection of what he knows about the skills measured? What should you do with his quiz result?

Discussion

Bill's low score is most likely an accurate reflection of what he knows; after all, he was absent for the instruction. Therefore, he did not have the *opportunity to learn* the skills he needed. Opportunity to learn is an important issue in measurement. Why would we give students a test to assess what we have not taught them?

This is a grave matter when students are being held accountable for test results, such as with graduation requirement tests. Students who have not been provided appropriate and relevant instruction cannot be held accountable for their performance. This is one reason why it is so essential for teachers to be intimately familiar with the objectives assessed on all such tests; and to teach the curriculum. Teachers who knowingly choose not to teach the curriculum they have been given could be betraying public trust and putting their students at risk.

Sometimes, however, students may be given a test containing some material they had not yet been taught to gather information on prior knowledge or what the students already know about a concept or topic. Collecting information on prior knowledge may expose students to material they have not yet been taught, but may provide the teacher with valuable information about what doesn't have to be taught, leaving more instructional time for more advanced skills. This is acceptable because the students are not being held accountable for their performance, and there are no negative consequences if they perform poorly because the teacher is using the results to plan instruction.

In Bill's case, his performance is expected to count in the calculation of his grade. But he did not have the opportunity to learn the material. Assuming that Bill's absence was legitimate, and he is not chronically absent, he probably should not have taken the quiz until he had been given some makeup work to complete. But because he did take the quiz, how should the results be used? Most important, Bill needs instruction in the content he missed, so he can continue to progress in algebra. A gap in his knowledge could easily hinder him in future classes. Therefore, some makeup work would be appropriate, as well as a makeup quiz. Bill's grade should not automatically be negatively impacted because he did not have the opportunity to learn. What are the teacher's options? Some teachers eliminate the top and bottom scores from a student's array of grades before calculating a final grade. (Remember the outliers from Chapter 3's discussion of mean scores?) This allows for a grade that is more likely to represent a student's actual performance.

Scenario Two—Don

You are the Testing Director for Sunnybrook School. Students at Sunnybrook must pass a state writing test to advance to the next grade level. Although most students will write their responses to the writing prompts by hand in the booklets, some special education students with specific disabilities will be allowed to construct their responses on their computer, as they do every day in the classroom, according to their special education plan.

To prepare for testing, you ask the special education team for a list of students who, according to their individual educational plans, are entitled to take the writing test using their computer. Don's name appears on the list, and you arrange for him to take the test on a computer. Just prior to testing, Don's teacher comes to you to ask why Don has been assigned to take the test in the computer room. You refer him to the list of students you have been given. He tells you that Don has never used a computer; in fact, he is not even familiar with the keyboard.

What should you do? If you require Don to take the test using the computer, will his score be valid? What if you don't allow Don to use the computer? Have his rights to an accommodation been violated?

Discussion

This situation is rare but will come up every so often, and it points out how important it is for teachers to be aware of the accommodations contained in their special education students' educational plans. It is especially likely to be a problem in schools with a high percentage of students in special education, each with a number of teachers and insufficient communication.

Accommodations are meant to "level the playing field" so that each student has an equal chance to show what they know and can do. An accommodation is not meant to give a student an advantage over others, but only to compensate for the disability. If a disability will interfere with a student's ability to perform, then an accommodation should be considered. The use of an accommodation can help ensure that students are given the chance to perform to the best of their abilities.

Your first consideration must be the student because this is a high-stakes test for him. You want the testing situation to be as comfortable and familiar as possible so that he can do his best on the test. Now would not be a good time to sit Don in front of a computer and require him to write for the first time using word processing. So what do we know about the validity of Don's score if he uses the computer? In this case, the accommodation could put him at a disadvantage instead of providing him a level playing field by compensating for his disability. However, if Don's writing skills are poor, whether or not he uses the computer may be unimportant—a low score would be valid. The problem is that if Don uses the computer for the first time and receives a low score, we will not know if it is because of his unfamiliarity with the way he was asked to respond; or because of weak writing skills.

Accommodations cannot be reserved for use during mandated assessments only. If the accommodation is truly necessary, it must be used during regular classroom instruction and assessment, as well as for standardized tests (if allowed). The problem here is that no matter what is done, an error has been made, and the school is at risk. The educational plan of a special education student is a legal document that must be followed by the school. If Don's plan said he needed the computer to write, then it is the school's responsibility to make sure he is given that opportunity every time he is asked to write. Don's rights to an accommodation have been violated all along. However, it is not fair to require Don to use a computer to write for a high-stakes test unless he is comfortable and familiar with the process. It would be better to consult with Don and his parents and test Don under conditions he is comfortable with. The school must begin to instruct and assess him using the computer (or revise his educational plan) immediately after the test is completed.

Scenario Three—Betty

Betty is a verbally fluent student. Up until now, most of the assessments she has taken in your music class were selected-response tests , so she rarely had to write and always received high grades. Because she is very verbal, she has had no difficulty participating in class discussions and answering questions in class. Recently, things in the school have changed, and students are being required to explain their thinking and provide other written responses. As the quarter progresses, you notice that Betty's performance in school has declined significantly. You decide to go back and look at some of her assessments to try to see what has gone wrong. Almost immediately, you notice that Betty is a poor writer. She cannot organize her ideas on paper. You reflect on her performance in your music class with a colleague who is Betty's science teacher. Betty seems to know the material in science class but has gotten poor scores on the assessments, she has been assigned to a low-achieving lab group and has become a behavior problem.

Are Betty's assessment scores valid? What might be some threats to validity? What might be done to address the problem?

Discussion

The key in this situation is that the format of the assessments has changed, and a weakness that did not affect this student's performance before (weak writing skills) may now be a major obstacle to allowing her to demonstrate what she knows. When Betty was answering multiple-choice questions, she did not have to write, and she was able to perform well. When the format of the assessments changed, her weak writing skills did not allow her to demonstrate her skills.

Unless Betty has suddenly stopped learning music and science, chances are her difficulties are because of the change in test formats. This would lead us to the conclusion that her assessment results are not a valid representation of what she knows about each subject. What has probably happened over the quarter is that Betty has become extremely frustrated with her inability to perform well on the science experiments. She has been moved to a lower-performing lab group and may have become bored. Boredom has resulted in behavior problems.

What can be done? First, Betty needs some direct instruction to improve her writing skills. This will most likely need to begin in language arts class, but her skills must be reinforced in her other classes too. In the meantime, Betty needs some accommodations in her assessments so that her teachers can find out what she knows about each content area. This would probably involve allowing Betty to dictate her responses to questions or take the test orally. Another option would be to allow Betty to write her own responses, but then give her the opportunity to explain them further. But what should happen to Betty's grades? Obviously, the school has changed its form of assessment, probably for a good reason. Betty's grades do need to reflect the fact that she cannot construct adequate responses to the questions of the science test. But, those assessment grades alone do not need to determine the group with which Betty works in the lab or the type of nonwriting instruction she receives. If she is learning the content in her courses, she needs help with writing, but she should not be put in a lower group. It is important to analyze what instruction is needed and provide that instruction.

This scenario also illustrates the power that observation and collaboration between and among teachers can have for the welfare of their students.

Scenario Four—Vincent

All of the elementary school teachers describe Vincent as a *typical boy*. He appears distracted in class, does not seem to be paying attention, and receives low grades. He rarely raises his hand and seems to try to hide from class participation. Vincent takes his first standardized test as a third grader. His scores are amazingly high compared to the grades on his report card. He receives scores in the 98th percentile in mathematics. His teachers are stunned. Are Vincent's test scores valid? If so, what could that mean for his classroom performance?

Discussion

Chances are very good that if proper standardized testing procedures were used, Vincent's scores are valid. We must consider the possibility that the teachers haven't *seen* this child and his abilities, a situation that happens all too often in classrooms. It is time for a one-on-one interview with Vincent, with the goal of allowing this bright little boy to enlighten his teachers—try to learn how he thinks, how he learns, and how he wants to be challenged!

Scenario Five—Margie

Margie is one of the brighter students in your class. She always does her homework, usually correctly. She receives good grades and generally performs well in class. But this assessment is different. Margie demonstrates almost no knowledge of the concept of inertia. Because the majority of the assessment covered physics, specifically inertia, Margie's score is very discrepant from her other performances.

Is Margie's score valid? Why or why not? What threats to validity may be at work?

Discussion

Sometimes bright student just don't perform well on a test, and sometimes they just don't get a concept. Any time students have any type of assessment results that are discrepant from other performances, it is worth asking the student if they have any ideas about what might have happened. Sometimes they just will not know. They might have had temporary test anxiety that paralyzed them. But sometimes, the students may have encountered a concept that they just found overly difficult. In that case, the scores are valid, but they signal a need for further instruction. The students will require a different instructional approach and some remedial work.

Scenario Six—The State Accountability Test

Your state administers an assessment to evaluate the effectiveness of each school. The results of the tests are used by each school to adjust and improve their instructional program. The testing occurs at one time each year, and because of test security issues, the test can only be administered to students in school each day of the administration. There are no makeup tests. Attendance is very important, however, because scores are reported as a percentage of students scoring at or above the satisfactory cut score. Because students who are absent for a day or more may not receive scores in all content areas, their scores will not contribute to the percent at or above satisfactory (In other words, they count as students not at the satisfactory level).

On a typical day, your school has no problems with students attending school. Therefore, attendance is not an issue being addressed by the school. However, this year, on the second day of testing the school receives news that a beloved teacher has passed away. Although the teacher had been ill for some time and not in school, the students and staff are obviously affected by the news.

The services for the teacher are scheduled for the fourth day of testing and almost two thirds of the students being tested are absent from school to attend the services with their parents. Although the district makes an appeal to the state to invalidate the test results, the state denies the request. Are these test results valid? Should the school use the test results to help them make decisions about the school's instructional program? Should the district use the scores to evaluate the school's performance? Why or why not?

Discussion

The school obviously believes that their scores on this year's test will not reflect their students' best work. When such a situation occurs, it is best to confront these issues prior to receiving the results of the test. It is helpful for those involved in testing to make notes of any observations of student participation and behaviors to assist the school in analyzing the results. Students may be distracted and not complete sections of the test, be unable to stay on task, or simply not be able to do their best. Based on their observations, teachers should be asked to predict the scores. If drops from the previous years are expected, it may be worthwhile to present this to the community.

When final results arrive, the school administrators must use the data they have gathered to decide if the results represent valid feedback about the instructional program at the school. If they do not have faith in the results, they should use other measures and indicators to assess their performance this year, and the district should do the same.

What to Do with Invalid Test Results

When you have decided that a test result is not valid, is the work an entire loss? Probably not, but it may take some original thinking to discover what you can learn! Have an open mind and ask yourself, What did the student show me on this test? Is he a good writer (even though he did not know much about the content)? Is she a good speller? Is this student willing to use advanced vocabulary, even though he can't spell those words yet? Does the student think creatively? Is this student distracted by the context of the problem? (Does she think too much, or read more into a problem than you intended?) Use what you discover in your future instructional plans for the student. For example, you may decide to use time generally devoted to emphasizing spelling to work on another weakness in the student who is a good speller. A minor adjustment in an assignment can meet this need.

Summary

Most of these scenarios involved the threats to validity for scores of individual students. Although some threats may actually occur with an entire group or subset of students (such as a poorly written item, vocabulary problems, etc.), the emphasis must be on evaluating the validity of the score for each student as an individual. Only then can the information really be useful to improve the academic performance of each student.

Hopefully through your study of threats to validity, you can see the importance of valid assessment data to inform your instructional decision making to meet the requirements of your state's NCLB program.

It may help to have some questions to guide your future analyses of assessment results. These questions can be used to consider the performance of a class or of an individual. If you go through this list, you've probably covered just about everything!

Questions to Guide Data Analysis—Individual Student Data

Are these the results I expected? Why or why not?

Are there multiple explanations for these results? (i.e., Are there threats to validity?)

- Do these results accurately represent what the student knows and can do?
- What do these results tell me about the effectiveness of my instruction of this student?

In what areas did the student do well? (What did the student show me he or she can do?)

If there is evidence of improvement, to what can it be attributed?

- How can I make sure the improvement continues?

If there is evidence of decline, to what can it be attributed?

- How can I reverse the decline?

In what areas did the student have difficulty?

- Does this weakness show up in other assessments?
- Do other teachers see this same weakness in this student?
- What can I do now to accelerate the student's learning?

What can I do so that this student's performance will improve?

- What is keeping this student from being more successful? How can I remove those barriers to his or her achievement?
- Do I see anything about the student's performance that could be easily addressed by instruction (i.e., simple errors or common misunderstanding)?
- How can I use the test results to show the student what he or she needs to do to improve?

Questions to Guide Data Analysis—Group Data

Did everyone participate in this assessment? Who was left out and why?

What percentage of the group performed at a satisfactory or better level?

Are these the results I expected, given this group's performance on other assessments?

- If no, did I use the same, consistent scoring standards?
- What could be other reasons for the discrepant results?
- What other data do I have about this group?

Is my class performing differently from those of other teachers in my grade level or course?

- How can those differences be explained?
- Do all of the teachers use the same scoring standards?

Did any specific groups perform better than others (e.g., boys versus girls, differences between ethnic and cultural groups, students at risk)?

Can I learn anything about my instruction for these groups?

- Are there patterns in the groups' performance that might help me plan more effective instruction for these groups?

A Note of Caution

You must be cautious about overinterpreting performance of groups with fewer than ten students. In Chapter 3, we looked at some mean (average scores) for a small group of students and noticed that a change in one score could result in a significant change in the group's average score. Therefore, with small groups, any outlier score (one higher or lower than the others) will affect the average of the group. When looking at the results of small groups, it is usually better to look at the results of the students as individuals to verify that each student is making progress and that one student making significant progress is not masking the information for the others.

A practical example might be as follows. Sometimes school improvement plans will have as a goal to improve the performance of a given group. This may put the teacher in the position of trying to compare the standardized test results of the current Hispanic students with the ones from last year. Everyone is happy when this year's group does quite a bit better than last year's group. That is, until someone points out that last year's group of six had four Hispanic students who had just entered the United States and only two who were born and raised here. This year's group of eight has six students who were born and raised here and only two who are struggling with language issues. Those differences alone could account for the apparent improvement in performance.

Now we will look at some actual student responses and practice diagnosing the weakness and prescribing the instruction to address them.

6

Using Assessment Results to Identify Instructional Needs

By now, you have probably noticed that one of the basic premises of this book is that teachers must emphasize the attention they give to *individual* student assessment results and the identification of individual instructional needs. This is also the foundation of the No Child Left Behind (NCLB) legislation. Remember that the legislation requires adequate yearly progress to be made by all students, as well as each of eight subgroups (racial groups and those with special needs). If you use the concepts you have learned in this book, and address each of your students' instructional needs, your students will be well on their way to meeting your state's NCLB requirements, and more important, to a successful future.

Once you have determined to the best of your ability that your students' assessment results are valid, it is time to look at these issues to decide what instruction is necessary to enable students to improve their performance. Wiggins (1994) discusses the problem of teachers not using data to drive their instruction. He notes that effective coaches watch for results and make adjustments in an ongoing fashion. Teachers must do the same if they want to enhance their students' performance. *The Results Fieldbook*, by Mike Schmoker, is a collection of descriptions of successful schools and school systems and how they got that designation. Each of these schools used data-driven decision making to impact their students' performance. According to Schmoker (2001), "When teachers regularly and collaboratively review assessment data for the purpose of improving practice to teach measurable achievement goals, something magical happens."

Fortunately, there has been considerable recent research on best or successful instructional strategies. This research gives teachers valuable information on what strategies to use to meet their students' instructional needs. Marzano (2003) included a chapter on instruction in his book *What Works in Schools: Translating Research Into Action*. This book also includes valuable chapters discussing the full realm of school effectiveness factors: school level, teacher level, and student level. This and other books like it will provide you with more in-depth information about how to meet your students needs than we will be able to cover in this chapter. Also, remember not to underestimate the value of collaboration with your colleagues.

In this chapter, we will explore some extensions of how student assessment results can be used to discover student instructional needs. Sometimes, student needs will be quite obvious, sometimes not. Test item or assignment format will limit what kinds of information you may get from your students' responses. For example, a constructed response may provide you with more details about your students' misconceptions than a true-false item, but well-constructed, multiple-choice items may provide you with some hints. Let's discuss a few of the areas you should consider to completely evaluate what your students are showing you they know and what they can do.

Making Observations

Some teachers will limit their evaluation of a student's work only to the rubric they are using (which will generally include knowledge of the content assessed, among some other criteria). Therefore, if they didn't intend to "count" grammar, and grammar is not in their rubric, they will not look at the student's use of grammar. Use of proper grammar will not be a part of the grade or feedback given to the student. This is only fair to the students who, hopefully, were told in advance about the criteria to be used for the evaluation of their work. But that does not mean that the astute teacher cannot make some observations about other skills the students may or may not have, whether those skills were intended to be assessed or not. Here are some areas in which you may want to make some observations that may help you focus future instruction. Obviously, you could not make these observations all at once!

Answering the Question

Some students may provide you with evidence that they have difficulty discerning what a question or assignment is asking them to do. Others may neglect to complete all steps of an assignment, focusing only on the first of several parts. These problems may keep students from demonstrating completely what they know.

Using Appropriate Vocabulary

When writing about a topic, students need to use appropriate vocabulary. Writing about science requires more precise language than writing for personal expression. Students should be able to use the language of the content area to demonstrate their knowledge (i.e., "numerator" instead of "the top number").

Sentence Structure and Language Mechanics

Although you may be interested only in the content of a response, you may get additional information by looking at a student's sophistication with sentence structure, capitalization, punctuation, usage, and spelling (use of compound sentences, ability to use quotation marks correctly, ability to set up a business letter, etc.). Of course, you cannot make these observations if students were asked to respond by making a list.

Organizational Skills

Students may include all of the content necessary to convince you they understand the topic assessed. But you may notice that their organizational skills are lacking, and their thoughts appear scattered.

Justification for Choices/Decisions

Some performance tasks will give students the chance to make a choice, choose a side, or present an opinion. Insight can be gathered by observing their ability to provide a justification for their choice or their ability to back up their choice with reasons, including sufficient details.

Quality of the Response

Rarely, a rubric will not focus on the quality of a student's response, but instead, for example, the number of reasons provided (i.e., give three reasons why…). Although this is not the best criterion to use, the opportunity to also consider the quality of those reasons should not be lost.

Proof the Text Was Read

Students will sometimes write responses to reading questions in such global ways that their answers lack evidence that they even read the text. Most of us have seen (and some of us may have written) that vague book report that may have gotten by even though it provides no real evidence the book was read. Look at your students' responses, and make sure that they provide sufficient details so that you have evidence to convince you that they have read the text.

Following Directions

An age-old complaint from teachers is that students do not follow directions. Sometimes this causes students to receive scores lower than they deserve, so the problem is definitely worth addressing in instruction. Failure to follow directions does not necessarily mean the student does not know the content being assessed.

Some Actual Student Responses

Now you will look at some actual assessment responses. Instead of providing you with the exact rubric that would be used for each assessment, let us assume we are evaluating the whole response. Therefore, you should practice looking at any and all aspects of the response for clues about the instructional needs of the student. Although these are all written responses, keep in mind that they could have been oral responses or even classroom conversations.

Before you read the discussion

☐ Study the response.

☐ Think about any obvious potential threats to validity.

☐ Provide a *diagnosis* or description of the student's weakness.

☐ Think about a possible *prescription* to address the weakness instructionally.

Because you do not have all of the information available to you that you would have if you actually taught these students, you may come up with a different diagnosis or prescription than the one discussed here. But that is fine, because the purpose of the exercise is to provide you with practice in this type of analysis, not to guarantee that you come to the same conclusion suggested here.

The examples of students' responses represent a variety of grade levels and content areas. They were chosen to illustrate *concepts* that will prove useful to you even if you do not teach that level or content. Remember that many of the examples have instructional implications for additional content areas. The responses are organized by some useful categories of types of information often available in student responses.

The Value of "Explain Your Answer"

Example 1

This response comes from the second part of a performance task about recycling. In a previous activity, the school has collected milk cartons to recycle.

> Your class is in charge of storing the cartons until they are taken to the recycling center.
>
> Your principal has found some space in a storage closet. The space is shaped like a rectangle. It is 12 feet by 9 feet. Your class decides

to block off your storage area by putting a fence around the edge of the space. How much fencing would your class need to have?

43 feet

Discussion

There is no obvious reason to question the validity of this answer. The question did not require the student to show her work, so some teachers, working with a scoring key indicating the correct answer is 42, would mark the answer as incorrect. The student's weakness could be in her math computation skills, in her ability to calculate a perimeter, or even in her ability to recognize that this was a perimeter problem. But, fortunately, the next question on this assessment asked the student to explain her answer. Read the response, and reconsider your initial response to the questions.

Write one or two sentences to explain how you determined the amount of fencing needed.

I add. I add 18 + 24 = 42. I add one more because I want to make sure there's enof fencing so I go 43.

It would seem as though this is a valid assessment of this student's knowledge of perimeter. There is sufficient evidence that she understood the question. In fact, she understood it so well that there is evidence she put herself in the situation described and went beyond calculating the perimeter and into the store to make a purchase! In her explanation, she provides evidence that she knows that it was a perimeter she needed to calculate, she knows the formula, and she was able to add correctly. She even provides evidence that she took a shortcut in her head and doubled the length of each side of the rectangle before she did her final calculation. Her explanation would be stronger if she were able to provide the details of her shortcut.

Chances are, if this assessment result is consistent with other data available about the student's knowledge of perimeters, she needs no further instruction on that topic. However, if the student had not been given the opportunity to explain how she obtained her answer, her answer may have been scored as incorrect. It would have been difficult to know how much she did not know. The explanation of her thinking adds to the information we have available to make our diagnosis.

This student may need some guidance as to how far to take the context of a test question. She will need some experience in choosing the one best answer when she is confronted by multiple-choice questions and making good decisions when she cannot explain her thinking. Her response could be improved with the addition of math terminology; that is, she should say that she is calculating perimeter and use terms like "length" and "width." Also, she needs practice providing specific details about her approach to problem solving and some attention to her spelling and writing.

Example 2

Students respond to the following question:

Shelia ate 1/3 of her pizza. Scott ate 2/9 of his pizza. Who ate more pizza? Explain your answer.

Student A:

Shelia ate more pizza because the fraction that is smaller is greater.

Student B:

Scott ate more because the numerator 2 is greater than the numerator 1. Also because the denominator 9 is greater than the denominator 3. Therefore, Scott ate more pizza than Shelia.

Student C:

I think Shelia ate a larger fraction of her pizza because 9 is larger than 3 and one fraction rule is when comparing fractions the fraction with the smaller numarator is greater.

Discussion

In this problem, the students needed to recognize that Shelia ate more pizza than Scott and explain how they knew this. A limitation of this question is that without the requirement of the explanation, the students have a 50/50 chance of answering correctly by guessing. This is another example of the importance of asking for an explanation and how much additional information that explanation provides.

For example, Student A might know that Shelia ate more pizza but can't provide a reason, so it may have been a lucky guess. It may be worth talking the problem through with Student A to see if help with math communication skills is all that is needed, or if the student really does not know how to compare fractions at all.

Student B knows how to communicate using mathematics terminology. He also knows that he must compare the numerator and the denominator to solve the problem, and he provides specifics. But he has his rules mixed up, which indicates he does not have a conceptual understanding, or he is not using number sense.

Student C may not understand what the numerator is, because she applied the rule for the numerators to the denominators. Or because she correctly identified Shelia as eating more pizza, she may have merely mislabeled the denominator in her explanation. Further assessment of this student will help the teacher decide what additional work she really needs.

The fact is, none of the students seem to get it. All three of these students need more work with manipulatives to help them see the origin of the rules they are using. They could be instructed in a flexible small group. Students B and C will probably be ready to move out of the small group before Student A because their understanding appears to be more advanced. Student A also needs help with providing explanations in mathematics.

Now let's consider Student D, who responds:

> I don't know who ate more pizza because I don't know the size of the two pizzas. If the two pizzas are equal, Shelia ate more, but if Scott's pizza is larger, I'm not sure.

This is not the expected response to this question, and the response requires processing on the part of the teacher. Some would simply mark it incorrect, but that would be doing a grave disservice to the student. This student obviously has a conceptual grasp of fractions beyond the intent of the question and probably needs some enrichment activities to continue enhancing his knowledge.

Recognizing Patterns in Responses

Example 3

These responses came from a multiple-choice test in language. This student got all of the other items correct; they were items assessing sentence structure, writing strategies, and editing of punctuation and capitalization.

Choose the best way to write the sentence:
A. The squirrel dig up the nut.
B. The squirrel dug up the nut.
C. The squirrel digged up the nut.
D. The squirrel dugged up the nut.
Student's response: C

A. Susie has went on vacation.
B. Susie have went on vacation.
C. Susie has gone on vacation.
D. Susie have gone on vacation.
Student's response: A

A. Cal swung the bat and hit the ball.
B. Cal swing the bat and hit the ball.
C. Cal swing the bat and hitted the ball.
D. Cal swung the bat and hitted the ball.
Student's response: B

Discussion

All of these items assess verb tense. The student answered all three incorrectly, which provides evidence of consistency, making it easier to assume that the student has difficulty with verb tense. We really don't have much information, however, just from looking at these items. It would be helpful to know if the student uses incorrect verb tense when speaking or writing his own sentences. From the items he answered correctly, we know he does well with sentence structure, writing strategies, capitalization, and punctuation.

At first glance, it appears this student will require instruction in verb tenses. But this is a case where the item format may be an issue. Multiple-choice questions require students to be able to see an error. Some students can have difficulty with this, especially if they know what the correct sentence should look like; their eyes may put it there for them.

It may be helpful to consider the type of instruction the student has had. This student's teacher reads sentences aloud to her class and asks the students if the grammar is correct or not. She has not asked them to read sentences to themselves, something they must do on the assessment. So we cannot tell if this is a valid assessment of this student or not. He may just need assistance reading for grammatical errors (editing), or he may require attention to his verb tenses in all areas: speaking, writing, and editing. Sometimes, assessment results will suggest more questions than they answer!

Hints about Learning Styles

Example 4

This response comes from a first grade mathematics assessment.

Four birds are sitting on a branch. Your friend throws a stone and scares one bird away. How many birds are left on the branch?

0

Discussion

We do not really have any information that would tell us that this response is not valid for this student. This student's answer suggests that she was not able to translate this question into a subtraction problem of 4–1 = 3. The answer 0 is incorrect. The student may have difficulty in understanding word problems and turning them into a number sentence, or she may not know her subtraction facts. Then again, perhaps she was unable to read the question.

Before planning future instruction, it might be useful to ask the student to show you, using manipulatives, how she obtained her answer. Actually, this student's teacher did just that, and here is the explanation she was given:

"Well, if one bird was scared and flew away, the others would fly away too. So there wouldn't be any birds left on the branch."

This new information is very helpful. We know the student was able to read and understand the question. Her explanation is typical for a field-dependent student. Students who are field-dependent (or field-sensitive) have difficulty separating the context of a problem from the question they are to answer; in other words, they consider the whole context and can become distracted by it. This student considered the entire situation and added additional knowledge she had to help her respond to the question. For her, this question never was about math, it was about the characteristics of birds that she had observed.

This question was ineffective for this student and thus resulted in an invalid response. The question could have been ineffective for other students in the class, too, and their invalid responses may be less obvious. The question could easily be rewritten to avoid this problem in the future by leaving out the thrown stone and the idea the birds were afraid. A better question would be the more direct one: "Four birds are sitting on a branch and one flies away. How many birds are left?" Of course, it may be preferential to leave animals out all together!

The student will require instruction on how to identify what a question is asking. We do not yet know if she knows how to subtract, or if she can translate a word problem into a math sentence. Additional assessment will be required to find this out. It will also be beneficial to this student (and others like her) if her teacher learns more about field-dependent learners, because their instructional needs can be quite different from their field-independent counterparts. A good resource for teachers about the learning styles of their students and the types of instruction that will be effective for them is *Comprehensive Multicultural Education*, by Christine Bennett (1990).

Example 5

Let's look at one more example from middle school integrated science and mathematics. Students used graph paper and a graphing calculator to plot the number of cricket chirps compared to air temperature. They were asked to make an inference about the line of best fit for the results.

> When we graphed cricket chirps to the increase in temperature, we found a positive correlation; that is, the higher the temperature, the more the cricket would chirp. Look at your scatter plot. When would the scatter plot of the chirps change? Consider both higher and lower temperatures. Would the graph become more positive or more negative?

Student A:

> The scatter plot of the chirps change when the tempeture increases or decreases. For example, if the temp. rises from 80 to 90 degrees or 50 to 40 degrees. The graph would become more positive if the temp increases because the warmer the temperature, the more chirps, But it could become negative if the temp decreases.

Student B:

> The scatterplot of the chirps will not have a positive correlation forever. I know this because animals cannot survive extreme temperatures and if is too hot or too cold the cricket will die. For example, if the temperature was 110 degrees a cricket may be in pain and would not chirp because it was too hot. This would cause the plot to be negative because the chirps would decrease. If the temperature went down, the chart would also go negative until it was so cold the cricket froze, then the chart would go negative to zero chirps and stay there.

Discussion

This is a challenging assessment meant to get at a student's ability to apply concepts. However, the student approaching the problem with purely a mathematical context will not do as well on this type of assessment as the student who is considering the entire context. In other words, this item may favor the field-dependent student.

Student A did not extend his answer to include the reality that eventually, as temperatures rose, the cricket would die. He has the general concept of the relationship between the variables but doesn't consider the context of the question to answer it completely. This student may be field-independent. He will need help with attending to the entire context of the question to develop his answers more fully. He could also use some help making his writing clearer.

Student B has considered the entire context of the question and taken it to the logical conclusion, that a cricket will not survive in all temperature ranges, so this affects his answer to the question. This student supplies a fairly complete answer and uses appropriate terminology (positive correlation). This student may be field-dependent because he considered the entire context of the question to answer it.

Evidence of Growth over Time

Example 6

Second grade students respond to the following prompt three times a year:

Each season brings with it many changes. Think about the things that we see, hear, and do during this season. Write a paragraph about the changes that are happening. After you have finished writing and checking your work, you are to draw a picture illustrating the changes in the season you just wrote about.

Because you are writing a paragraph, be sure it has the following:

☐ All sentences written with details

☐ A clear topic sentence

☐ At least three supporting-details sentences

☐ A concluding sentence

☐ Indented paragraph form

☐ Words spelled as best you can

☐ Correct punctuation

Here is a student's first response in the fall (the pretest):

Changes in fall

The changes in fall are pepol raking lefse and kids jumping in lefse The farms are harvfsting crops. Bras are flying southa regtiels are hibernating. Thst how fall begens and ends

Discussion

This student knows some things about changes in fall and understood the prompt, so this is most likely a valid assessment of his writing skills. This student clearly needs help in developing ideas and elaborating on details. He also needs help with beginning and ending a paragraph and obviously, his spelling.

The teacher of this student's class conferred with every student about his or her writing. The teacher established a goal and an action plan based on the expectations she had for the students' writing. She taught the class how to turn their ideas and phrases into sentences and provided opportunities for the students to practice. She gave students paragraphs that were missing topic sentences, and the students wrote topic sentences for the paragraphs. They also thought of topics of interest and wrote topic sentences for each. Students shared their topic sentences with each other and discussed them. Let's look at what the same student wrote just three months later:

Changes in Winter

These are some of the changes in witer. One of my changes are when you go outside it is a good time to go skiing, sledding and snowbording because thar is snow on the ground. Another thing changing in winter is basketball begins because it is an in door sport and outdoors sports are ending. We drink hot chocolate so we can warm up after we paly out side. I really liket making this paragraph because I like winter.

Discussion

Obviously, this second grade boy made a lot of progress in his writing. His ideas on the second paragraph were much more developed, he used descriptive language, he included elaboration using facts and details, and he used beginning and ending sentences. His sentences were also more complex than his first attempt. Punctuation improved, and he learned to indent. His teacher continued to help him develop his writing, and continue to work on his spelling and grammar. Here is the student's final response of the year:

Changes from Spring to Summer

From spring to summer we have changes that we hear, see, and do. Fist, kids have summer vacation for three months because kids need a break from school. Another change is when you stay outside at night, you will see fire flies because it is too cold for bugs to come out in other seasons. A third change is there is more daylight than black because the sun is closer to us. I think spring and summer are my favorite seasons because they are warm.

The student had improved his grammar and spelling and used proper punctuation. His topic sentence was more fully developed, and his ideas were more elaborated. The improvement in this student's writing was significant for a second grader, and he entered third grade with good basic writing skills that can be easily developed further. His parents and his next teacher could easily see the progress he has made because of the teacher's attention to documenting growth over time.

The students in this class were also evaluated on their skills at writing dictated sentences three times during the year: September, January, and May. A checklist was used to indicate if the student demonstrated each skill frequently, sometimes, or not yet. Examples of skills assessed were

♦ Capitalizes the beginning letter in each sentence
♦ Uses ending punctuation marks
♦ Capitalizes days of the week
♦ Uses a comma to separate city and state
♦ Capitalizes other proper nouns, and so on

This list provided students and parents with the list of skills students were expected to demonstrate in their writing. The three evaluations over the school year provided data about how students had progressed over the school year.

The Attempt

Example 7

Students responded to the following task:

Some people think 1 and $\frac{1}{4}$ is a larger share than 1 and $\frac{1}{3}$.

Some people think 1 and $\frac{1}{3}$ is a larger share than 1 and $\frac{1}{4}$.

Which share do you think is bigger? Write a letter to a second grader. Tell why you are right. Use drawings to explain your thinking. Remember that a second grader must understand what you write.

Figure 6.1. Which Share Is Bigger?

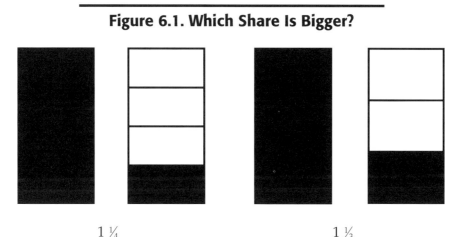

1 $\frac{1}{4}$ 1 $\frac{1}{3}$

I think that 1 and 1/4 is bigger because then you could get a bigger piece. You would be able to share with one person and you could get the biggest piece.

Discussion

One of the first things you may have noticed about this response is that the student did not attend to the directions. She has not written a letter at all. The student was able to draw a picture of 1 $\frac{1}{4}$ and 1 $\frac{1}{3}$ correctly (see Figure 6.1) but still does not know that 1 $\frac{1}{3}$ is bigger than 1 $\frac{1}{4}$. Particularly, she does not know that the denominator equals the number of parts, and a larger denominator does not mean a larger piece.

Her explanation has no substance. Her teacher plans to reteach her fractions using manipulatives to help the student build conceptual understanding. Then she must work on the student's mathematics communication skills, perhaps by starting with oral explanations, and moving on to written ones. This student will also need some reminders to read the directions she is given and perhaps, learn to circle some of the words that tell her what to do (e.g., write a letter).

Example 8

Students read an informational piece about the Chesapeake Bay and fish ladders. They were asked a series of questions about their reading.

> If you visited around the bay, how might the information in this article be useful to you? Include at least two ideas in your response that are based on the information in the article.

> If I visited around the bay, it will be cool and pretty. First I would try to learn more about them and take pictures. For example, it will be cool to see all of the things and expespecialy the bay. Finally, I really want to see the Chesapeake Bay. Another example, is you always have to obey the fishing laws. These are two reasons that I want to visit the Bay.

From this student's response, you can't really be sure she read the text. She makes general statements and uses nonspecific words (cool, them, things). She doesn't address the question at all, and instead of referring to information she may use from the article, she provides reasons she wants to visit the Bay and labels them as examples. This student uses "finally" inappropriately. She obviously knows she should begin her response with a topic sentence and end it with a concluding sentence.

We really don't know about this student's ability to read and understand the article. We do know that she needs tremendous help with organizing her ideas, developing her ideas into specific details, and referring back to the text. The use of graphic organizers may be of great help to this student as she learns to respond to these types of questions.

Example 9

Middle school students read a story and respond to some questions.

> One interpretation of the story is that Taroo is courageous. What evidence is there in the story to support the interpretation that Taroo is courageous? Find and explain three pieces of evidence from the story that support this interpretation.

The evidence in the text is he talks with the girl and tells her the story that he is there enemy tribe.

Discussion

The student did find one piece of evidence, although he did not explain it in detail. However, we know he knows what evidence is. He neglected to complete the assignment, so we do not know if he forgot the question asked him for three pieces of evidence, or if he could only identify one. A middle school student should have better spelling and usage skills. This student's teacher plans to assess his ability to identify three pieces of evidence and explain them orally and devise an appropriate instructional plan based on her findings. She will also provide more guidance in the areas of editing and developing details in the student's writing.

Giving Students Choices

Example 10

Your friend has pieces of an apple pie. She gives you the choice of having $\frac{1}{3}$ of the pie or $\frac{1}{4}$ of the pie. Which would you choose? Explain the reason for your choice.

I would choose the smaller piece. One reason for my thinking is that the $\frac{1}{3}$ is the smaller pieces. 2nd reason is that $\frac{1}{4}$ is the larger pieces. 3rd reason for my thinking is that I do not like apple pie. 4th reason is that I would not like the bigger pieces. The 5th reason for my thinking is that if you color in what than $\frac{1}{4}$ is larger than $\frac{1}{3}$.

Discussion

This student has the same conceptual misunderstanding as the student in Example 7. However, the instructional implications for this student are a little different because when asked for a reason, she supplies five (only one of which is reasonable or correct). This student may have been taught somewhere to give as many reasons as possible, the more the better, with little regard to quality.

An interesting twist to this question is that it does allow for students to make a choice; therefore, some students will pick the bigger piece, but some will pick the smaller piece. The teacher must be flexible enough in scoring to provide equal credit for either choice as long as the reasoning is correct (which it is not, in this case). Students need to understand that their scores are not based on their choices, but they are based on the accuracy and completeness of their support of their answers.

Discovering Possible Learning Disabilities

Example 11

Students read a story and were given the following assignment:

> Name two character traits that Alaster seems to have. Support your choices with evidence from the text.

> One character trait about Alastor is evil, because he poisoned the king so the king would hate all the people instead of Alastor. Another character trait is that Alastor is greedy, because when the king died, Alastor told Sir Simion that he had succeeded as king.

Discussion

This is actually a well-developed response to the question. It is complete, contains details from the story to support the character traits chosen, and uses correct grammar, spelling, and punctuation. The teacher would probably want to provide this student with more challenging texts and questions to stretch and develop his skills. But look at another response from the same class:

> One chahates orchit about Klasn is evill because he poioind The lening so the lening would hate all the people insead fof playins he desidin to go play in the attic and the anotheor character is the sir simon one of the friends that william has and he is going to fit king Alaster.

Discussion

The inconsistencies in the writing of this student clearly indicate a problem. The response is not at all organized, and the errors in spelling and sentence construction and lack of punctuation make it difficult to understand. However, there are hints that the student understood parts of the story and knows what character traits are. He seems to have identified the trait of evil and relates it to poisoning.

This student's teacher plans to give him the opportunity to respond to this question orally to help her decide if the problem is reading and writing or just writing. In any case, further, more extensive assessments are necessary, perhaps even to diagnose a possible disability.

Using Student Responses to Improve Your Assessments

Example 12

Students were to follow the rules of a game and decide if it is fair.

You and two friends decide to create a game tossing pennies. You decide to toss two pennies. If both come up heads, one person gets a point. If both come up tails, the second person gets a point. If one penny comes up heads, and the other comes up tails, the third person gets a point. You decide that the person with the most points after 25 tosses is the winner.

First, play the game with two friends, then answer the following question.

Is this a fair game? Explain your answer. Draw charts or diagrams if it will help.

> I think that it's fair because we all had a fair chace of winning. We all had a fair chance of winning because we all won twices.

Discussion

This student may or may not understand what a fair game is, and the student does not know that this game, as written, is not fair for all players. The student does not understand probability and could not even list the possible outcomes for each toss (heads-heads, tails-tails, heads-tails, tails-heads) to see that the one heads and one tails outcome would occur twice as often as the other two. It is also interesting that the student reports each of the three players won twice, because that would have required the game to have been played six times (150 coin tosses). This student also needs a lot of help communicating about mathematics in a written format. He offers no rationale for his answer, so we do not know how much he really understands.

The teacher needs to review the concept of fair games and may want to conduct the experiment with the group of students not understanding the concept while recording the results for them to see. This is also a wonderful opportunity to modify an assessment to improve it. The teacher may want to require the students to record all possible outcomes, as well as their actual observations, as part of the task to make sure students have data with which to make their decision.

Using Assessment Results for Instructional Grouping

Example 13

Students were given a set of subtraction problems to assess their ability to subtract with regrouping. Figure 6.2 shows examples of the same items for three students. Correct answers are circled.

Figure 6.2. Subtraction Problems

	980	438	249	384	776
Student A	−252	−229	−168	−92	−285
	732	211	121	312	511

	980	438	249	384	776
Student B	−252	−229	−168	−92	−285
	628	208	(81)	282	(491)

	980	438	249	384	776
Student C	−252	−229	−168	−92	−285
	732	(209)	91	(292)	511

Discussion

Student A definitely has a strategy and definitely can't subtract with regrouping. He very accurately subtracts the smaller digit from the larger one and does this independently in each column. His facts are good, but he does not understand regrouping, and therefore he needs major work on that concept.

Student B seems to have a beginning grasp of the concept of regrouping, but makes computational errors that could be related to regrouping (i.e., she is off by 100). She did get two of the items correct.

Student C also answered two items correctly, but he has a tendency to do the same thing as Student A. After a small group review of regrouping using manipulatives to help them with the concepts, all three of these students were able to correct their work. While Students A, B, and C participated in their small group, other students in their class worked on problem-solving activities.

An alternative strategy to having students solve all of the problems would be to ask them to circle all of the problems that require regrouping. This teaches students to look at the problem before they begin to solve it, while allowing the teacher a quick way to find out which students don't understand regrouping.

Example 14

One school used assessment results to diagnose and prescribe instruction for their students in need. Almost halfway through the school year, a fourth grade team noticed that a large number of students were reading below grade level. The criteria they used to determine grade-level reading were ability to decode grade level text, ability to respond to a reading question orally, and ability to respond to a reading question in writing. The team hypothesized that the criteria actually identified students in various stages of reading development or tiers.

They developed a common assessment tool to help them identify which students fell into which tiers. They scored the assessments as a group to make sure they all used the same standards, using a rubric that had been developed for the assessment. The team was able to establish cutoff scores and use the assessment results to identify students with similar instructional needs. These students were divided into groups and received specific instruction based on these needs.

Tier I readers participated in special programs to accelerate their attainment of reading decoding skills. Tier II students received specific instruction in comprehension strategies with focused instruction in both oral and written comprehension with an early emphasis on the oral piece. Tier III students had instruction focused on improving written responses to grade level text through modeling, guided practice to learn how to form a developed response, frequent opportunities to practice their new skills, and focused feedback on their responses.

The goal of the team was to make sure that each student progressed, and the teachers used similar assessments to document growth as the year progressed.

Learning from Correct Answers

Example 15

The marmot, the largest member of the squirrel family, has a body that is twice as long as its tail. How long is the tail of a marmot whose total length is 54 cm? Explain.

Student A:

The marmot's tail is 18 cm long. I found out by dividing 54/3 and got 18. That is my answer.

Student B:

The marmot's tail is 18 cm long because if you divide 54 by 3 you get 18 so if you add 18 + 18 you have ⅔ which stands for the body and 18 cm left which stands for the tail.

Student C:

His tail is 18 cm long. I got this by dividing 54 cm by 3 because there are 3 parts to his body. The body is two parts and the tail is one part.

Discussion

All of these students arrived at the correct answer. And surely that is a relief to any teacher! But instead of stopping there, this teacher uses other aspects of the assessment to search for information the students have given her about their instructional needs, some of which may be unrelated to the topic of this assessment. This approach will allow the students to sharpen their skills.

Student A does not explain why he divided by 3 but does write in complete sentences. He needs help in unpacking his thinking (describing his problem-solving process). Student B writes a run-on sentence, but begins to make the point that she understands that the body was 2/3 of the total length of the marmot. She needs some help with her sentence structure and how to more clearly describe her thought process. Student C concisely explains why he divided by 3.

Example 16

A high school math teacher gave her students the following problem.

Directions:

Support your answers with appropriate mathematics information.

Use the space provided to write your response.

Eileen just got a job typing term papers. She charges $20 plus $2 per page.

Give an equation that represents the amount she charges in terms of the number of pages.

Find the amount she charges for a 10-page paper.

Student A:

amount charged total = y   pages typed = x

y = 2x + 20 y = 2(10) + 20

y = 20 + 20

y = 40

Student B:

Eileen charges $20 plus $2 per page which equals y = $2x + $20, x equaling the amount of pages, y equaling total cost of the term paper. If a person gave Eileen a 10 page report it would cost him $40 because it is $2 times the amount of pages which equals $20, plus the standard $20 which comes to a total of $40. So if a person gave Eileen a 10 page term paper he has to cough up the $40 but if I were you I would type it myself.

Discussion

Obviously, both of these students understood the problem and were able to provide correct answers. The differences between the answers may simply amount to personal style. Student A is definitely brief and to the point. Her answer could have been improved with the addition of a $ sign label for the total charged, but she did complete the requirements of the task. Student B, however, is a writer, providing lots of detail into her thought process, although no more actual information than Student A. Student B adds an evaluation of the problem by commenting that she did not think that Eileen' services were a bargain.

The important point here is that students with very different types of answers can still meet the requirements of an assignment. The tendency may be to grade Student B more generously, but Student A's response is also worthy of a high grade. Student B may have gone above and beyond what was asked for, but it was not necessary. Student A met the requirements of the assignment by reducing it to a simple algebra problem. The length of a written response may not be related to the quality of the response; that is, more is not always better!

Looking at Levels of Understanding

Example 17

How do you know that 18 is 82 percent of 22? Include a proof or equation with your explanation.

Student A:

> I know that 18 is 82 percent of 22 because 82 percent as a decimal is .82. If you multiply .82 times 22 you would get 18.04 and then round and you get 18. Also, 82 percent as a fraction is 82/100 and 22/1. If you multiply them yoo get 18.04, round and you get 18. Therefore, 18 (82/100 × 22/1 = 1804/100 = 18.04) is 82 percent of 22.

Student B:

> I know that 18 is 82 percent of 22 because you can use proportion to prove it. Because percents are out of 100 you write a proportion showing 18 is to 22 as x is to 100, like this
>
> 18/22 = x/100
>
> After this, you just have to work the proportion, 1800/22 = 81.81 and because we know the decimal will be repeating, we can round 81.81 to 82. That is why 18 is 82 percent of 22.

Student C:

> I know that 18 is 82 percent of 22 because the way to get the answer is an equasion, to get the answer you would write x × 22 = 18. The x representing the percent. You would divide both numbers (18 and 22) by 22. The 18 when divided by 22 will be .82 is 82 percent. Therefore that is why I know that 18 is 82 percent of 22.

Student D:

> I know that 18 is 82 percent of 22 because if you write this in a pro-portion was it would equal 18/22 therefore if this keeps on going and going you would round it to 18. So 18 is 82 percent of 22.

Discussion

This entire class's assignments could be grouped into three groups for in-struction because they represent three levels of understanding. Students A and B represent group 1. These students understood their lesson in finding percent when both the whole and the part are known. They use their own words to describe their process, although each one has chosen a different way. They are probably ready to move on in their math lessons.

Student C represents group 2. These are students who understood the les-son in a very literal way. They can apply the exact process they learned, but it is unclear if they have mastered the concepts because they have used the exact language of their lesson with no elaboration or words of their own. They still need some extensions into authentic applications and more practice with the skill.

Student D represents the group 3, the one that didn't learn the concept. This student has some of the vocabulary, but this group will need a lot of work to get the students to the point where they will understand the concept well enough to be able to answer this question. Because some of them did not even attempt this question, they may have difficulty with more basic questions such as these: What is 82 percent of 22? 18 is what percent of 22? 18 is 82 percent of what number?

Example 18

This assignment was used as a warm-up to assess student understanding of concepts taught the previous day.

1. Are congruent figures also similar figures? Explain.
2. Are similar figures also congruent figures? Explain.
3. Suppose you are replacing a broken window. Should it be a congruent window or a similar window?

Student A:

1. Congruent figures are not similair because it only has the size and shape.
2. Similair figures are congruent because it has size, color, and shape just like the thing.
3. If I was going to replacing a broken window I think it should be similair because if you replace it with congruent the window would look different.

Student B:

1. Yes, they are because congruent is the same shape and size, and similar is the shape but not the size.
2. Similar figures can be congruent, but they don't have to be. They can be the same shape but not the size, then they would be similar, but not congruent.
3. It should be similar because it has to fit.

Student C:

1. Congruent figures are similar because similar figures have the same shape, and to be congruent figures must have the same size and shape.
2. Similar figures have the same shape but they don't have to be the same size, so they aren't always congruent, but if they were the same size, they would be congruent as well as similar.

3. The window must be congruent because to fit correctly it has to be the same size and shape of the broken window.

Discussion

This is an effective warm-up activity because it supplies the teacher with information about basic understanding of the concepts as well as the ability to apply them. From the results of the warm-up, the teacher can quickly see differing levels of understanding among the students. Student A does not seem to have grasped the concepts of similar and congruent figures (including the spelling of "similar"), and therefore she cannot apply the concepts in question three. She will need significant work on these concepts, hopefully using a different approach than the one used previously, because that approach was obviously not successful. Student B understood the concepts and can repeat the definitions he was taught but cannot apply the concepts to the problem in question three. Student B will need some review and practice applying the concepts. Student C understood the concepts and can apply them. Perhaps Student C could be further challenged by teaching the application to Student B!

When You Don't Get What You Expected

Example 19

The following writing assignment was given to a fifth grade music class that had just completed a unit on theme and variation.

> Pretend that you are the author of a music textbook for fifth graders. Write a paragraph to introduce theme and variations form. It should be easy to understand and should make readers interested in learning more about this form of music. Your paragraph should

1. Define theme and variation.
2. Suggest two or three ways a composer can change a theme to create a variation.
3. Recommend one piece of music which is an example of theme and variations form. Give the title and composer. Add any information that might interest your readers in the piece.

Student A:

> Theme and variations the first thing is that variation is on "America." It is by Charles Ives. Variations on "Simple Gifts." It is by Aaron Copland. This is about theme and variations. The End.

Student B:

> Theme and variations are a type of symbol in music. Two ways composer can change the vartion is he can change the music. Simple Gifts by Aaron Copland.

Discussion

These two student responses were representative of the entire class. These students could not successfully respond to a task with multiple parts. They tended to answer the last part of the question that they read. Furthermore, it would appear that the students cannot explain theme and variation, although they have obviously learned about two pieces of music.

First, their teacher must give them additional instruction in attending to multistep tasks. In the meantime, simpler assessments may result in better information. It may be necessary to completely reteach theme and variation and assess the students on their understanding of the concepts before asking them to apply it.

Example 20

The media teacher read a book to second graders and asked them to answer the following:

> Another student is looking at the book *Berlioz the Bear*, by Jan Brett. By looking at the pictures, he thinks he would like the story, but he wants to know more about it and the borders on the pages. Write a paragraph to tell him about Jan Brett's illustrations. Be sure to tell what she shows in the borders. Also, tell where she got the ideas for some of her designs and for the character of Berlioz.

Very few of the second graders were able to answer this question. It required too many different pieces of information and was too involved for them. The teacher will need to simplify the task by making it more focused on one aspect of the book, that is, what does the author show in the borders of her illustrations? Then, after the concepts have been assessed, the teacher will need to begin work on teaching students to respond to all parts of a question, but now she knows that her students are at a beginning level with this skill. They will need to be taught some strategies to help them check to make sure that they have answered a question completely, and the complexity of their questions must be increased according to what is developmentally appropriate for them.

Being Flexible

Sometimes, your students' assessments will tell you that what you are doing is not really working. Consider the case of an elementary school where the second grade teacher found serious gaps in her students' ability to read. Because reading is a basic skill that is a prerequisite for success in all other content areas, her school found a way to restructure their schedule so that the children having difficulty could have an additional 30 minutes per day of reading instruction. They also increased the amount of adult support available to students during their regular reading instruction and while they worked independently on their reading. This meant that other classrooms in the school had to give up some of their staff and work with larger student groups to invest this time with the second graders. However, the payoff justified the sacrifices because the third-grade teachers are going to receive a class of grade-level readers next year. Student needs cannot always be addressed in the time available for the majority of students to learn. It is these times that the good schools will find ways to get students what they need to progress.

Summary

We could have studied example after example of student assessment results that indicate instructional needs. We have all seen the students who have the answer correct but don't label it in centimeters, quarts, and so on. We are frustrated by the students who ignore the context of the problem and say we'll need 4.35 buses for the field trip. We see students doing a wonderful job of graphing data without ever labeling an axis or providing a title. They write well-constructed essays without capitalization, missing or incorrect punctuation, or use of proper spelling. Others write with accurate punctuation and spelling but don't express a single detailed idea. All of these students are demonstrating a lot of knowledge that needs to be fine-tuned and expanded by instruction. It is a big job, and the only way to be efficient, provide the instruction needed, and not waste precious time on what the students already know is to carefully analyze what your students are showing you they know and can do. The key to that is the accurate and thorough processing of the students' assessment results by their teacher.

An excellent resource to help a teacher learn more about the misconceptions students have is *Understanding by Design,* by Grant Wiggins and Jay McTighe. The book is included in the bibliography. Wiggins and McTighe provide a useful framework for how to assess student understanding and how to teach so that students will develop deep understanding. These authors also provide some additional information on how teachers can be fooled by student responses, and how we tend to make assumptions that may be flawed about what students know or the level of their understanding.

Wrap Up

Hopefully, this book can continue to serve you as a resource and reminder of the important measurement concepts you must be aware of as a prerequisite to using assessment results in planning your instruction. Approach assessment results with questions. Always remember to question the reliability and validity of your information for each and every student, and be sure to follow up with additional data when you have discrepant or incomplete information. Listen to what your students are telling you whenever you assess their learning.

We have explored the concepts of assessment from the federal mandated down to the most important, the individual student. It was the purpose of this book to provoke new ideas about current issues in assessment. It was an attempt to encourage teachers in their search for more time and efficiency in their classrooms so that they can cover that ever-expanding curriculum, while preparing students to do their best on any test they may face. Perhaps some of the tips in this book will prove useful in your attempt to be a better teacher today than you were yesterday, and a better teacher tomorrow than you were today.

Now that you are more comfortable with basic measurement concepts, some possible threats to the validity of your students' assessment results, and how to use the information for instructional planning, you are more prepared than ever to be the teacher your students remember as the one who made them a success as a learner, the teacher who left no child behind.

References

Bennett, C. (1990). *Comprehensive multicultural education* (2nd ed.). Boston: Allyn and Bacon.

Marzano, R. J. (2003). *What works in schools, translating research into action.* Alexandria, VA: Association for Supervisions and Curriculum Development.

Schmoker, M. (2001). *The results fieldbook, practical strategies from dramatically improved schools.* Alexandria, VA: Association for Supervisions and Curriculum Development.

Wiggins, G. (1994). None of the above. *The Executive Educator, 16*(7), 14–18.

Bibliography

Assessment—General

Ellis, A. K. (2001). *Teaching, learning, and assessment together.* Larchmont, NY: Eye on Education. (Includes a collection of "reflective assessment strategies" which will assist any teacher in learning what students have learned.)

Kreisman, S., Knoll, M., & Melchoir, T. (1995). Toward more authentic assessment. In A. Costa & B. Kallick (Eds.), *Assessment in the learning organization: Shifting the paradigm* (pp. 114–138). Alexandria, VA: Association for Supervision and Curriculum Development. (One high school's experience with the transition to authentic assessment. Includes reflections of how teachers decided what to teach based on how they would be assessing student performance.)

Marzano, R. J., Pickering, D. J., & McTighe, J. (1993). *Assessing student outcomes: Performance assessment using the dimensions of learning model.* Alexandria, VA: Association for Supervision and Curriculum Development. (Includes sample performance tasks.)

McTighe, J., & Ferrara, S. (1997). *Assessing learning in the classroom.* Washington, DC: National Education Association.

Stiggins, R. J. (2001). *Student-involved classroom assessment* (3rd ed.). Upper Saddle River, NJ: Merrill Prentice Hall. (An extremely well-written, practical guide to effective classroom assessment. Includes sections on test item development, scoring, interpretation, and communication, with a special emphasis on student involvement in their own assessment. Provides guidelines for the use and development of many types of test items.)

Wiggins, G. (1993). *Assessing student performance: Exploring the purpose and limits of testing.* San Francisco: Jossey-Bass.

Wiggins, G., & McTighe, J. (1998). *Understanding by design.* Alexandria, VA: Association for Supervision and Curriculum Development. (Wiggins and McTighe present a framework for teachers to use to assess student understanding through performance assessment. They provide methods to determine the appropriate types of instruction to meet the stated goals of the instruction, and the complementing assessment to determine student understanding. This book contains thoughtful discussions of what understanding is and how to determine what are the most important concepts for students to understand.)

Developing, Scoring, and Using Performance Assessments

Danielson, C., & Hansen, P. (1999). *A collection of performance tasks and rubrics: Primary school mathematics.* Larchmont, NY: Eye on Education. (Tips for how to write and adapt tasks and rubrics; provides sample tasks and rubrics for primary mathematics assessment. This author also has a version for upper elementary mathematics, middle school mathematics, and high school mathematics.)

Glatthorn, A. A. (1999). *Performance standards and authentic learning.* Larchmont, NY: Eye on Education. (A good basic "a to z" reference for incorporating authentic assessment and instruction.)

Swartz, R. (1995). Developing writing prompts for assessing thinking and content learning in science classrooms. In A. Costa & B. Kallick (Eds.), *Assessment in the learning organization: Shifting the paradigm* (pp. 75–83). Alexandria, VA: Association for Supervision and Curriculum Development. (Some basic guidance in helping science teachers make the switch from traditional assessment to assessment of critical thinking skills.)

Stiggins, R. J. (2001). *Student-involved classroom assessment* (3rd ed.). Upper Saddle River, NJ: Merrill Prentice Hall.

Wiggins, G., & McTighe, J. (1998). *Understanding by design.* Alexandria, VA: Association for Supervision and Curriculum Development.

Writing Good Assessments/Test Items

Ebel, R. L., & Frisbie, D. A. (1991). *Essentials of educational measurement* (5th ed.). Englewood Cliffs, NJ: Prentice Hall. (Good sections on test planning, constructing true-false, multiple-choice, and other objective items, as well as essay.)

Osterlind, S. J. (1997). *Constructing test items: Multiple-choice, constructed response, performance and other formats.* St. Paul, VA: Assessment Systems Corporation.

Wiersma, W., & Juro, S. G. (1990). *Educational measurement and testing* (2nd ed.). Boston, MA: Allyn and Bacon. (Useful sections on test construction, selected and constructed response items.)

Scoring and Rubrics

Danielson, C., & Hansen, P. (1999). *A collection of performance tasks and rubrics: Primary school mathematics.* Larchmont, NY: Eye on Education. (Tips for how to write and adapt tasks and rubrics; provides sample tasks and rubrics for primary mathematics assessment. This author also has a version for upper elementary mathematics, middle school mathematics, and high school mathematics.)

Marzano, R. J., Pickering, D. J., & McTighe, J. (1993). *Assessing student outcomes: Performance assessment using the dimensions of learning model.* Alexandria, VA: Association for Supervision and Curriculum Development. (Includes many samples of rubrics.)

Using Assessment Data and Grading

Marzano, R. J. (2000). *Transforming classroom grading.* Alexandria, VA: Association for Supervision and Curriculum Development. (A thoughtful discussion of grading with the assumption that the purpose is to provide students and parents with feedback; can be a little technical.)

Stiggins, R. J. (2001). *Student-involved classroom assessment* (3rd ed.). Upper Saddle River, NJ: Merrill Prentice Hall.

Wiggins, G., & McTighe, J. (1998). *Understanding by design.* Alexandria, VA: Association for Supervision and Curriculum Development.

School Improvement

Marzano, R. J. (2003). *What works in schools.* Alexandria, VA: Association for Supervision and Curriculum Development. (A summary of the school-level, teacher-level, and student-level factors that contribute to student achievement. Practical and easy to read.)

Schmoker, M. (1999). *Results* (2nd ed.). Alexandria, VA: Association for Supervision and Curriculum Development. (A series of examples of successful schools and how they got that way.)

Schmoker, M. (2001). *The results fieldbook.* Alexandria, VA: Association for Supervision and Curriculum Development. (Vignettes describing the school improvement process at successful schools.)

Whitaker, T. (2004). *What great teachers do differently: 14 things that matter most.* Larchmont, NY: Eye on Education. (Practical guide to improving teacher performance, fun and easy to read.)

Index